*Taking Laughter Seriously*

# Taking Laughter Seriously

John Morreall
Department of Philosophy
Northwestern University

State University of New York · Albany

Published by
State University of New York Press, Albany

©1983 State University of New York

Printed in the United States of America

For information, address State University of New York
Press, State University Plaza, Albany, N.Y., 12246


Library of Congress Cataloging in Publication Data
Morreall, John, 1947–
    Taking laughter seriously.
    1. Laughter.    I. Title.
BF575.L3M65    1982            152.4            82-5858
ISBN 0-87395-642-7                              AACR2
ISBN 0-87395-643-5 (pbk.)


10   9   8   7   6

*For Lynne, who got me laughing again*

# Contents

# Preface

I⊤ is a curious fact that although thousands of books and articles have appeared in our century dealing with human emotions and related phenomena, by far the greater number of these have been concerned with such things as fear and anger and anxiety. Relatively little has been said about more positive phenomena like laughter. If we consider the close connection between psychology and the treatment of mental problems, perhaps this imbalance should not surprise us. Nonetheless, we cannot hope to have anything like a complete picture of human life until we pay attention to such things as laughter.

But until a few years ago, the study of laughter was treated in academic circles as frivolous. Because laughter is not a serious activity, the unstated argument seemed to run, it is not possible to take a serious interest in it; and so anyone proclaiming an interest in studying laughter probably just wants to goof off. This argument is invalid, of course. The fact that laughter and humor involve a nonserious attitude does not imply that we cannot adopt a serious attitude toward examining them. Nor does the nonserious attitude in laughter and humor render them somehow unimportant as features of human life, and therefore unworthy of our attention. Indeed, as I will try to show, our capacity to laugh is anything but a peripheral aspect of human life, and to understand our laughter is to go a long way toward understanding our humanity.

The last few years have seen, at least in psychology, a changed, more positive attitude toward the study of laughter. But for all the empirical research which has been done, there have been very few attempts to construct a comprehensive theory of laughter and humor. And the recent theories that have been formulated have in most cases suffered from the same lack of rigor which made traditional theories unacceptable. What is needed most urgently at this point in the investigation is not more piecemeal studies on various small aspects of laughter and humor, but a general account of laughter and humor and how they fit into human life. This account must be formulated in terms specific enough to give the theory some explanatory power; but must not, as past theories have done, simply take one kind of laughter and claim that all cases of laughter are really of that kind. What is needed, in short, is a *philosophical* examination— philosophical in the narrower sense that it will be theoretical, and rigorously so, and philosophical in the wider sense that it will locate laughter in the human experience. It is such an examination that I hope to provide in this book.

I am grateful to the editor of the *Journal of Aesthetic Education* for permission to use parts of my article "Humor and Aesthetic Education," which appeared in Vol. 15, No. 1 (1981) of that journal; to the editor of *Proceedings of the Eighth LACUS Forum* (Columbia, S.C.: Hornbeam Press, 1982) for permission to use parts of my "Language, Logic, and Laughter"; and to the editor of *Philosophical Studies* for permission to use parts of my "A New Theory of Laughter," which will appear in late 1982. The editors of *The New Yorker* kindly gave me permission to use the Arnie Levin cartoon in Ch. 4 and the Charles Addams cartoon in Ch. 6.

A number of colleagues and friends have my thanks for their comments on and corrections of earlier versions of this book—most especially, Lynne Blom, Samuel Todes, Paul Teller, Mike Martin, John Deigh, Doug Lindsey, Mark Coppenger, and Ted DeWelles. Lastly, I am grateful to Kathleen Gefell Centola, who gave me encouragement and help, to Dave and Pete Huse, who first got me wondering what laughter is, and to Lillian Morreall, who has always been there to laugh at my stuff.

# 1

# Can There Be a Theory of Laughter?

In the first century the Roman Quintilian complained that no one had yet explained what laughter is, though many had tried.[1] And even with all the philosophers and psychologists who have tackled the problem in the intervening centuries, the story is pretty much the same today—we are still without an adequate general theory of laughter. The major difficulty here is that we laugh in such diverse situations that it seems difficult, if not impossible, to come up with a single formula that will cover all cases of laughter. What could all of the following cases—and this is a relatively short list—have in common?

*Nonhumorous laughter situations*
Tickling
Peekaboo (in babies)
Being tossed and caught (babies)
Seeing a magic trick
Regaining safety after being in danger
Solving a puzzle or problem
Winning an athletic contest or a game

*Humorous laughter situations*
Hearing a joke
Listening to someone ruin a joke
Watching someone who doesn't get a joke
Watching a practical joke played on someone
Seeing someone in odd-looking clothes
Seeing adult twins dressed alike

Running into an old friend on the street

Discovering that one has won a lottery

Anticipating some enjoyable activity

Feeling embarrassed

Hysteria

Breathing nitrous oxide

Seeing someone mimic someone else

Seeing other people experience misfortune

Hearing outlandish boasting or "tall tales"

Hearing clever insults

Hearing triple rhymes or excessive alliteration

Hearing spoonerisms and puns

Hearing a child use some adult phrase correctly

Simply feeling in a silly mood and laughing at just about anything

Now this list could certainly be shortened by grouping some of the items under more general headings. We might lump joke telling and practical jokes together as jokes, for example, or we might make up a more general heading which covers both winning a contest and solving a puzzle. But is there some heading under which we might accommodate such diverse cases as winning a contest and being tickled?

Part of the difficulty in finding the "essence" of laughter, if indeed there is such a thing, is that it is not at all clear how to even categorize laughter among human emotions and behavior. When we look at the psychological and philosophical literature on fear or love, we find different approaches, of course, but there is agreement over the basics. Fear, for example, is an emotion connected with perceived imminent harm—theorists have agreed on at least that much since Aristotle. And they also agree that fear is connected with our actions inasmuch as it is connected with the impulse to flee. Ethologists like Konrad Lorenz have studied how fear is related to "fight or flight" mechanisms in animals, and much of this research yields insights that help us understand fear in humans. Further, we can study the physiology of the fearful state along with its ethology to gain some understanding of how fear has had survival value for other species and for our own, and thus how it has fit into evolution.

When we look at theories of laughter, on the other hand, we find no such agreement on the basics. Some have classified laughter as an emotion, while others have insisted that laughter is incompatible with emotion. While it seems correct to say that, properly speaking, laughter is a piece of behavior and not an emotion, it is obvious that laughter is not a behavior like yawning or coughing, which is to be explained only physiologically. Somehow laughter is connected with emotions—we laugh with glee, with scorn, with giddiness, etc. But just what is this connection?

There are difficulties, too, in trying to relate laughter to human action. Fear leads to flight, but there seems to be no action that laughter leads to. And studying animal emotion and behavior does not help here, for only a very few animals exhibit behavior that is even roughly similar to human laughter, and then it is only in reaction to such simple stimuli as tickling.

If we ask about the survival value of laughter and how it might have evolved, we also run into problems. Indeed, many have suggested that laughter does not have survival value and that it could only be disadvantageous to a species in which it evolved. Laughter often involves major physiological disturbances. There is an interruption of breathing and the loss of muscle tone; in heavy laughter there may be a loss of muscle control—the person's legs may buckle, he may involuntarily urinate, etc. If the traits that are preserved in a species are those which have survival value, how could something like laughter have been preserved in our species?

As we set out to understand laughter, then, we stand forewarned not only of the great diversity of situations in which it occurs, but of the anomalous character of the behavior itself.

We will start our examination by considering the three traditional theories of laughter. Each lacks comprehensiveness, as we shall see, but each is valuable in calling our attention to a kind of laughter which must be accounted for when we try to construct a comprehensive theory.

# 2

# The Superiority Theory

THE oldest, and probably still most widespread theory of laughter is that laughter is an expression of a person's feelings of superiority over other people. This theory goes back at least as far as Plato, for whom the proper object of laughter is human evil and folly.[1] What makes a person laughable, according to Plato, is self-ignorance. The laughable person is the one who thinks of himself as wealthier, better looking, more virtuous, or wiser than he really is.[2] Now we enjoy laughing at such people, but our laughter involves a certain malice toward them, and malice is a harmful thing, a "pain in the soul" Plato calls it. In laughing, furthermore, our attention is focused on vice. We should not cultivate laughter, he argues, lest some of what we are laughing at rub off on us. In heavy laughter, too, we lose rational control of ourselves, and so become less than fully human.

Plato was especially opposed to conventionalized laughter as in comedies; indeed, he claims that it is harmful even to portray people as laughing in literature. "Men of worth must not be represented as overcome by laughter, and still less should we allow such a representation of the gods."[3] In the *Laws* he is somewhat less harsh. It is valuable to know what ugliness looks like, the Athenian stranger (who seems to represent Plato's point of view) says, and so the portrayal of ugliness in comedy can have a certain educational func-

4

tion. Nonetheless, there is always the danger of comedy having a morally damaging effect, and so no citizen should spend much time watching or reading comedies—certainly he should never act in a comedy.[4] Where the writing and performance of comedy are allowed, there should be strict censorship to insure that no citizen is ever held up to laughter.[5]

Aristotle agreed with Plato that laughter is basically a form of derision. Even wit, he says, is really educated insolence.[6] Now because people do not like to be laughed at, laughter can serve as a social corrective to get wrongdoers back into line. But this value of laughter should not be overrated. Since in laughing we are concerned with what is base, Aristotle insists, too much laughter is incompatible with living a good life. He also says that the joking attitude can be harmful to a person's character inasmuch as it makes him nonserious about important things. In the *Nicomachean Ethics* he discusses how the person who laughs too much strays from the ethically desirable mean.[7] "Those who carry humor to excess are thought to be vulgar buffoons. They try to be funny at any cost, and aim more at raising a laugh than at saying what is proper and at avoiding pain to the butt of their jokes." Aristotle does not condemn the humorous attitude entirely, however; he admits that "those who would not say anything funny themselves, and who are annoyed at those who do, seem to be boorish and dour." What is called for is moderation, but this is seldom achieved. "Most people enjoy amusement and jesting more than they should . . . a jest is a kind of mockery, and lawgivers forbid some kinds of mockery—perhaps they ought to have forbidden some kinds of jesting."

The superiority theory as presented by Plato and Aristotle was influential on subsequent thought about laughter, though little was added to the theory until the early modern period when Hobbes put it into a stronger form. For Hobbes the human race is a collection of individuals in constant struggle with one another. "I put for a general inclination of all mankind, a perpetual and restless desire of Power after Power, that ceaseth only in Death," he wrote in his *Leviathan.*[8] Laughter comes in when we are winning in the struggle. It expresses, according to Hobbes, "a sudden glory arising from some conception of some eminency in ourselves, by comparison with the infirmity of others, or with our own formerly."[9] Laughter, then, is self-congrat-

5

ulatory; it is based on our finding ourselves better off in the struggle of all against all than someone else is, or than we used to be.

Like Plato and Aristotle, Hobbes was concerned that laughter could be harmful to a person's character. There is something wrong, he felt, with the person who can feel good about himself only by looking down on others. He admits that a person can laugh not from any explicit comparison of himself with others, but merely from "a sudden conception of some ability in himself."[10] Still, he feels that most laughter is at others, and so is a sign of pusillanimity.

> [Laughter] . . . is incident most to them, that are conscious of the fewest abilities in themselves; who are forced to keep themselves in their own favour, by observing the imperfections of other men. And therefore much laughter at the defects of others, is a signe of Pusillanimity. For of great minds, one of the proper workes is, to help and free others from scorn; and compare themselves onely with the most able.[11]

Hobbes's account of laughter became the classic form of the superiority theory, and it has been defended many times in the last three centuries. An interesting recent development is the attempt to understand laughter in an evolutionary way as arising from aggressive gestures found in early humans. The ethologist Konrad Lorenz, for example, sees laughter as a controlled form of aggression,[12] and many theorists have been ready with suggestions as to how the physical behavior of laughing shows that laughter evolved from aggressive gestures and still retains this hostile character.

In *The Secret of Laughter*, Anthony Ludovici gives an evolutionary version of Hobbes's theory of "sudden glory"; all laughter, he says, is an expression of a person's feeling of "superior adaptation" to some specific situation, or to his environment in general.[13] Laughter takes the physical form it does, the baring of the teeth, because originally laughter was a physical challenge or threat to an enemy. This showing of the teeth in laughter, as in the aggressive behavior of dogs, is a way of asserting one's physical prowess. In laughter, Ludovici says, it is our way of telling the enemy that we are strong and better adapted to the situation than he is. We still feel threatened when someone laughs at us, much as when an animal bares its teeth at us, because the laugher is putting himself in the position of an enemy challenging our position. As humans developed, of course,

6

there were more ways in which one person could be superior to another than just in physical prowess, and so the claim to superior adaptation in laughter came to focus not just on strength or agility, but also on cleverness, intelligence generally, or wealth. We can see this development in the race paralleled in the development of the individual today, according to Ludovici: the first thing that children laugh at is the physical maladaptations of others, while later they come to also laugh at mental and cultural maladaptations.[14]

Another attempt to trace the evolution of laughter from hostile physical gestures is Albert Rapp's *The Origins of Wit and Humor*.[15] All laughter, according to Rapp, has developed from one primitive behavior, "the roar of triumph in an ancient jungle duel."[16] This vocalization of triumph was probably so early in human development, he says, that it came before there was language. And not only would the individual combatant who was victorious laugh in triumph, but if his kin were standing on the sidelines, they would join in the laughter too. In this way, Rapp suggests, citing Donald Hayworth, laughter may have come to serve as "a vocal signal to other members of the group that they might relax with safety."[17]

The next step in the evolution of modern laughter was the development of ridicule. Originally people laughed at the black eye and the broken arm of the defeated combatant, but later they came to laugh outside of combat situations at any mark of injury or even deformity because these suggested that the person *had* been defeated in combat, or perhaps, in the case of deformity, that he *would* be. In this way we came to laugh at those who had not attacked us, but who had suffered some misfortune or who were deformed in some way. Frailty, deformity, and error, Rapp says, are "modern substitutes for the battered appearance of one's defeated opponent which once triggered triumph laughter."[18] Even today, he points out, we shun being laughed at for some deformity of ours or for some mistake we have made, just as we shun being laughed at for having been defeated. Indeed, people have been killed for laughing at other people just as they have been for physically attacking them.

In modern humor this element of ridicule is not always obvious, Rapp admits, but that is because we sometimes add to the ridicule an affectionate, benevolent attitude toward the person being laughed at. In genial humor, the "laughter is ridicule tempered with love. When directed toward a child, it takes the form of mild amusement at weakness or predicament, plus a large quantity of affection. When directed toward a Tom Sawyer or Falstaff it is still laughing *at* weakness, error, deformity, or predicament in a character toward whom you feel affection."[19]

The final achievement in the development of ridicule into its various modern forms in humor is laughter at oneself. The feeling of superiority is still present when you laugh at yourself, Rapp says; what you are ridiculing is a "picture of yourself in a certain predicament."[20] In laughing at yourself, the part of you that is laughing has dissociated itself from the part of you that is being laughed at.

Rapp also sees the need for his superiority theory to account for such things as puns and witty nonsense, which evoke laughter but which do not seem to be based on ridicule. I will save a discussion of these, however, until I come to my criticisms of the superiority theory. But before offering my own criticisms, I should note one line of response that has been directed against the superiority theory at least since its formulation by Hobbes. This response consists in simply denying that laughter can be derisive. "Laughter," Voltaire wrote, "always arises from a gaiety of disposition, absolutely incompatible with contempt and indignation."[21] And in this century we have had writers like Max Eastman suggest that we "dismiss from the topic of laughter at the outset the topic of scorn."[22]

What is wrong with this response to the superiority theory is that it denies an obvious fact—that people sometimes laugh in derision at other people. Perhaps we feel that no one *should* do so, but we must not confuse normative questions with factual ones. In point of fact, people often laugh at the misfortunes of others, and seem to have done so throughout recorded history. Surely the Romans who came to the Colosseum to enjoy watching Christians mauled by lions laughed precisely at the suffering and death of those in the arena. And although Christian civilization was supposed to make people more sensitive than pagans to the suffering of others, still public torture and executions were a popular source of amusement through the Middle Ages and into our own "enlightened" centuries. There is a record from the late Middle Ages of the citizens of the town of Mons buying a condemned criminal from a neighboring town so that they could have the fun of quartering him themselves. Even in

Voltaire's day it was common for the rich to amuse themselves by taking a coach to an insane asylum to taunt the inmates.

World literature from its earliest days has made many references to the laugh of derision. It is found several times in the *Iliad,* for example, and is almost the only kind of laughter found in the Bible. In the *First Book of Kings* (18:30) we are told that Elijah taunted the priests of Baal, ridiculing their gods as powerless compared with Yahweh. After deriding them, he has them slain. In the *Second Book of Kings* (2:23) the prophet Elisha is met by a group of children who taunt him for his baldness. So great an offense is this derision to the prophet that he curses the children in the name of the Lord, and immediately two bears come out of the woods to mangle them.

To modern Western ears these passages seem cruel, but that is only because of our relatively recent moral objections to the enjoyment of others' suffering. We should keep in mind, too, that our objections to cruel laughter are not, even today, part of all cultures. Alfred North Whitehead related the following story: "Some of our fellows who were out in Africa . . . during the war tell of how the Negroes went down to a stream for something and came back roaring with laughter. What was the joke? Why, a crocodile had suddenly popped out of the water and snatched one of their fellows off."[23] In cultures like Samoa cruel laughter and the laugh of ridicule seem to be the dominant kinds of laughter. Among the Greenland Eskimo, contests of ridicule were once their only judicial procedure, even for such offenses as murder. Someone who had a complaint against another challenged him to a contest before the clan or tribe in which they took turns ridiculing each other. There was no distinction made between defensible accusations and mere slander; the parties were even allowed to snort in their opponent's face or tie him to a tent pole. All that counted was who got more laughs at his opponent's expense. That person was declared the winner by the assembly, and if the shame of the loser was great enough he and his family were ostracized from the community.[24]

And we need not travel to Greenland to find derisive laughter; our own children, and ourselves as youngsters, show a remarkable capacity for ridicule. Some children who have been speaking for only a few years are already proficient at making up nicknames with which to taunt other children and adults who have physical deformities, or whose clothing, language, or behavior is different from their own. And studies have shown that what young children find most amusing is someone else's suffering.[25] It takes a lot of exposure to different kinds of people and ways of life for children to become tolerant of customs, styles of dress, etc., that are not their own. It also takes time and moral training for children to develop a sensitivity to the suffering of others, so that they will be distressed, and not amused, by suffering. As Piaget and others have shown, children do not start out with the awareness that other people are subjects like themselves—this is something they must learn.

A good deal of the natural human propensity to derisive laughter is still left in most adults, I would submit. Our moral training has removed some of it, but it still comes out in many ways, in the glee we feel at the suffering of someone who has wronged us, for example, or in our laughter at ethnic jokes. Even if it is not permissible to laugh at someone's misfortunes in polite company, we still enjoy witty repartee, especially well-phrased insults. Comedians like Don Rickles have built very successful careers not on telling jokes, but simply on singling people out of the audience and mocking them in great detail about their race, accent, clothing, ugliness, etc. The worst manifestation of our taste for this kind of laughter is probably the pitifully childish "situation comedies" that have glutted our television schedules for the past decade or so, many of which have almost no plot but consist simply of a group of family members or friends trading obvious and stupid insults.

It would be foolish, then, to respond to the Hobbesian theory of laughter by denying the reality of derisive laughter. A more reasonable line of criticism, I think, is to show that not all cases of laughter can be explained as involving feelings of superiority, and hence that "sudden glory" cannot be the essence of laughter.

If we look at our list of laughter situations in Chapter 1, we find many that do not fit into the superiority theory. The laughter of the baby, for instance, at being tickled, or at the game of peekaboo, cannot be attributed to a sense of superiority in the baby, because these kinds of laughter begin before the baby has any image of itself in comparison with others, indeed before the baby even distinguishes itself as a being separate from its surroundings.

Older children and adults do evaluate themselves and are capable of a sense of superiority. But in many situations where we laugh, there need be no feelings of superiority. Adults can laugh, like infants, at being tickled, and they can laugh at seeing a magic trick, or at running into an old friend on the street. No self-evaluation has to be involved in any of these cases; indeed if there is self-evaluation in the case of laughing while watching the magic trick, the person laughing would have to judge himself *inferior* to the magician who has succeeded in tricking him.

As with the above cases of nonhumorous laughter, so too with humorous laughter—there are many instances of laughter that involves no feelings of superiority. Much merely verbal humor, as in someone's use of a triple rhyme or excessive alliteration to get a laugh, is not directed at anyone and requires no self-evaluation. Many puns, too, are mere verbal play, and are not designed to evoke feelings of superiority.

Absurd or nonsense humor often makes us laugh without involving us in any self-evaluation. Someone for a joke once put a bowling ball in my refrigerator while I was not home. When I next went to the refrigerator and opened the door I broke out laughing. But not *at* anyone, and not out of any feeling of superiority—I was simply amused by the sight of this object in a completely inappropriate place. Indeed, we sometimes enjoy absurdities of this type not only without feelings of superiority, but even in situations that show us up as inferior in some way. I occasionally get out of bed and make my breakfast before I am fully awake. On one such occasion I remember bringing the coffee pot over to the table from the stove and proceeding to pour about a cup of coffee onto my cornflakes before I snapped to what I was doing. I instantly broke into a laugh. The absurdity of what I had done not only did not enhance my self-esteem in this situation; it detracted from it. Now sometimes people produce a forced laugh upon making a mistake in social situations, in order to appear comfortable in the situation and to forestall harsh criticism. But this was not the case here—I was alone and my laughter was sincere. I was simply enjoying the silliness of what I had done.

There are even people who enjoy sharing with others laughter at their own blunders. I have a friend who once ran out of gas in a tiny foreign car he had just bought. He got the car off onto the shoulder of the road and set off on foot for a gas station. But when he returned with a can of gas, he couldn't figure out where to put it into the car. He eventually opened the hood and found what appeared to be the right spout. He unscrewed the cap and poured in the gallon of gas. In fact this was the radiator, and so now not only would the car not start, but he had gasoline instead of just water in the cooling system. This was a costly mistake, both in time and money, but he found it very funny at the time. And ever since he has enjoyed telling the story of this blunder, or having someone else tell it. He doesn't have some deep-seated need to punish himself or to have his friends laugh at him. Nor does he tell the story in "self-glory" by comparing himself today with his former self; he freely admits that he's still so unmechanically minded that he could make a similar mistake tomorrow.

Proponents of the superiority theory like Rapp would say that in cases like the above there is still the feeling of superiority, but what the laugher is ridiculing is a picture of himself dissociated from the self who is laughing. "What happens, in effect, is: a person learns to regard himself as though he were someone else. . . He then proceeds to smile amiably and objectively at the antics and predicaments which accrue to his *alter ego.*"[26] This explanation, however, seems ad hoc. Granted that sometimes in laughing at ourselves, e.g., in laughing at pictures of ourselves as children, we may be laughing at an alter ego with which we do not fully identify ourselves, this need not be the case. Often in laughing at our blunders, I think, we laugh *harder* because it is our very selves—the ones who are laughing—who made the blunder. In laughing at myself for pouring the coffee over the cornflakes, I know that I laughed especially hard because I did *not* dissociate myself from the groggy person who had made the silly mistake. And I think I know my friend well enough to say that he would not enjoy the story of the gas being put into the radiator half as much if he thought of the bungler who did this as anyone other than himself.

Even if the superiority theory didn't have these cases of laughing at oneself to explain, moreover, it would still have to account for our laughter at incongruity where no one is being ridiculed, a good example of which is the bowling ball in the refrigerator. Hobbes acknowledged that our laughter is sometimes triggered by incongruities, but he tried to stick to the superiority theory by maintaining that "laughter without offense must be at absurdities and infirmities abstracted from persons."[27] But what is the force of "at" here once we are no longer talking about laughing at persons? We laugh at, that is ridicule, persons in the superiority theory when we feel superior to them in physical prowess, intelligence, or some other human feature, and prompted by this feeling show a contemptuous lack of respect for them in our actions. In this sense of "laugh at" we cannot laugh at anything other than a person, or something which we can treat as a person, since we can compare ourselves to, and so feel superior to, only things of our kind, namely, other persons. We cannot ridicule inanimate objects, or situations. We can mock a person indirectly, if you will, by seemingly abusing some object connected with him. We might get a group of people to laugh at a fat person in his absence, for example, by parading around with his oversize coat, emphasizing how large it is to accommodate his belly. But here we are not mocking the coat, we're using the coat to mock the person.

We do speak of "laughing at" absurd situations like the bowling ball in the refrigerator, of course, but only in the sense that we are amused by the absurd situation. And this sense of "laugh at" carries no connotations of ridicule, feelings of superiority, or even self-evaluation. We cannot feel superior to or ridicule the bowling ball in the refrigerator, in short, and so Hobbes is guilty of equivocation if he thinks that our "laughing at" incongruous situations such as this is the kind of "laughing at" required by his superiority theory.

At least some of those who have espoused the superiority theory, I think, have been led into thinking that laughter must involve positive self-evaluation because in laughing we are enjoying ourselves, we are feeling good. It is important to see here that the fact that a person is feeling good does not mean that he is necessarily feeling good *about himself* (the expression "enjoy oneself" is misleading in this regard), still less that he is comparing himself to others, or to some earlier state of his own. The mistake here is similar to that sometimes made in ethics when the possibility of altruism is denied on the grounds that since actions are always done by agents who (in some sense) *want to* do those actions, all actions are done *for the benefit* of the agents doing them. What this reasoning overlooks is that someone might well have as the object of his wanting the benefit of another person, with no explicit or implicit reference being made to his own benefit. Similarly someone can feel good laughing without focusing on himself at all. Laughter need not be self-evaluative any more than action need be self-serving.

Our general conclusion about the superiority theory, then, is that it could not serve as a comprehensive theory of laughter, for there are cases of both humorous and nonhumorous laughter that do not involve feelings of superiority.

# 3

# The Incongruity Theory

IN turning now to our second theory of laughter, the incongruity theory, we shift our focus from the emotional or feeling side of laughter to the cognitive or thinking side. While amusement for the superiority theory is primarily affective—it is self-glory or the feeling of triumph—for the incongruity theory amusement is an intellectual reaction to something that is unexpected, illogical, or inappropriate in some other way. In both theories there is a certain duality or contrast that triggers laughter, but the superiority theory makes the overly restricted claim that this duality must be between the laugher's evaluation of his own importance and his evaluation of someone else's importance (or his own formerly). And as we have seen, this claim is shown false in many cases of laughter. The incongruity theory, on the other hand, though it does not deny that feelings of superiority may be involved in laughter, does not see the duality in laughter as necessarily taking the form of a contrast between the laugher's sense of his own importance and his evaluation of someone else. Instead this theory works with the more general notion of incongruity.

The basic idea behind the incongruity theory is very general and quite simple. We live in an orderly world, where we have come to expect certain patterns among things, their properties, events, etc.

We laugh when we experience something that doesn't fit into these patterns. As Pascal put it, "Nothing produces laughter more than a surprising disproportion between that which one expects and that which one sees."[1]

The incongruity theory was first hinted at by Aristotle; though because it did not fit in with the superiority theory of his *Poetics* and *Nicomachean Ethics*, he never developed it. His recognition of incongruity as a source of laughter occurs in the *Rhetoric*, where he points out that one way for a speaker to get a laugh is to set up a certain expectation in his listeners and then to hit them with something they did not expect. As an example he cites a line from an unknown comedy: "And as he walked, beneath his feet were—chilblains."[2] The same result, Aristotle notes, is also produced by jokes that depend on a change of spelling or word play.

Because Aristotle said no more about incongruity as a source of laughter, the idea was not even mentioned by most of those who commented on his work. The exception was Cicero, who repeated what Aristotle said about getting a laugh by surprising your listeners, but then went on to try to assimilate this kind of laughter into Aristotle's superiority theory.

The incongruity theory was not to be worked out in any detail until the eighteenth and nineteenth centuries, where its most famous proponents were Kant and Schopenhauer. Kant's theory of laughter is not simply an incongruity theory; it involves the notion of an emotional release, and so also comes under our third heading, "Relief Theories," which we will discuss in Chapter 4. But the idea of incongruity plays a central role in Kant's account of laughter, and so is worthy of our consideration here. "In everything that is to excite a lively convulsive laugh," Kant says, "there must be something absurd (in which the Understanding, therefore, can find no satisfaction). *Laughter is an affection arising from the sudden transformation of a strained expectation into nothing.*"[3] Kant offers several examples of jokes, among them the following:

> The heir of a rich relative wished to arrange for an imposing funeral, but he lamented that he could not properly succeed; "for" (said he) "the more money I give my mourners to look sad, the more cheerful they look!" When we hear this story we laugh loud, and the reason is that an expectation is suddenly transformed into nothing. We must note

16

well that it does not transform itself into the positive opposite of an expected object—for then there would still be something, which might even be a cause of grief—but it must be transformed into nothing.[4]

Schopenhauer's version of the incongruity theory is somewhat different from Kant's. He says that what we get in the punch line of a joke or in other laughter situations is not, as Kant claimed, *nothing*; our expectations are not simply frustrated and that is the end of the matter. Rather we get something that we were not expecting. Whatever it is, it completes the story or fits into the situation in some way—it just does not fit in the expected or "normal" way.[5] In Kant's joke about the mourners, for example, we do not, as we listen, set up a specific expectation which is simply transformed into nothing. In hearing that the heir was lamenting his inability to arrange a lavish funeral, we form a general expectation that some kind of explanation will be given for this fact in the rest of the story. And what follows *is* an explanation. What makes this a joke and not simply a story is not that no explanation is given for the heir's frustration, but that the state of affairs appealed to in the explanation is incongruous. Professional mourners are expected to be able to look sad on cue, so a group of them who couldn't hide their pleasure with their high pay would be odd mourners indeed.

If the explanation given in the story were an ordinary one, such as "These April rains will ruin the procession," then there would be no joke at all. On the other hand, if *no* explanation were given, if our expectation that somehow the heir's frustration would be accounted for were simply "transformed into nothing," then there would likewise be no joke. If the story, say, ended after telling us that the heir lamented his inability to arrange for an imposing funeral, we would have frustrated expectation but would be unlikely to laugh.

In Schopenhauer's own account of laughter, he says that there must be an incongruity between a concept—which by its very nature is general and lumps together unique, individual things as if they were identical instantiations of that concept—and those things themselves. "The cause of laughter in every case is simply the sudden perception of the incongruity between a concept and the real objects which have been thought through it in some relation, and laughter itself is just the expression of this incongruity."[6] What causes laughter, if you will, is a mismatch between conceptual understanding and perception.

Having looked briefly at two versions of the incongruity theory, we can now turn to a general evaluation of the theory. Leaving aside individual difficulties which Kant's, Schopenhauer's, or other versions might face, I think that the central weakness of the incongruity theory is that it is not comprehensive enough to explain all cases of laughter. As long as we are considering only cases of humorous laughter, the theory works well—indeed later I'll appeal to incongruity as part of the mechanism of all humor. But there are many cases of nonhumorous laughter which do not involve incongruity.

One theorist who realized the limitations of the incongruity theory was Kant's contemporary, James Beattie. In his own account of laughter Beattie appeals to incongruity, and he uses much the same language as Kant and Schopenhauer, but he makes it clear that only some laughter is to be explained by appeal to incongruity. He distinguishes between what he calls "sentimental laughter," the kind involved in humor, and "animal laughter." The former "always proceeds from a sentiment or emotion, excited in the mind, in consequence of certain objects or ideas being presented to it. . ."[7] And it is incongruity in the laughter stimulus that causes this sentimental laughter; this laughter "seems to arise from the view of things incongruous united in the same assemblage."[8] Or in more long-winded fashion he says that the cause of humorous laughter is "two or more inconsistent, unsuitable, or incongruous parts or circumstances, considered as united in one complex object or assemblage, as acquiring a sort of mutual relation from the peculiar manner in which the mind takes notice of them."[9]

The second kind of laughter Beattie mentions, "animal laughter," does not work at this intellectual a level, and he does not propose to analyze it in terms of incongruity; indeed he devotes only a few sentences to it. Animal laughter, Beattie says, "arises, not from any sentiment, or perception of ludicrous ideas, but from some bodily feeling, or sudden impulse, on what is called the animal spirits, proceeding, or seeming to proceed, from the operation of causes purely material."[10] Animal laughter is the kind found in babies, who have no intellectual capacity for appreciating incongruity; it is their response to stimuli such as tickling. In adults too we find animal laughter "occasioned by tickling or gladness."[11]

In Chapter 5 I will discuss in detail the difference between humorous and nonhumorous kinds of laughter, but here we need only note Beattie's point that at least some types of nonhumorous laughter are not to be explained in terms of incongruity. Incongruity is an intellectual or conceptual matter, and the psychological mechanism behind, say, the laugh of tickling, is simply not this sophisticated. We should add here, too, that there are cases of laughter that do involve intellectual understanding but do not involve incongruity. When we laugh on solving a puzzle, for example, or on seeing the perfectly executed acrobatic stunt, this is not mere "animal laughter," but we need not make any judgment of incongruity here. So incongruity is not behind even all cases of what Beattie calls "sentimental laughter."

Beattie adds another important qualification to the claim that laughter is a reaction to incongruity. Not all incongruity that a person notices will trigger laughter, he says. Incongruity will not excite what he calls the "risible emotion" when our perception of incongruity is "attended with some other emotion of greater authority."[12] And this is an important feature of laughter often overlooked in overly intellectual formulations of the incongruity theory. Laughter, even in humor, is not merely an intellectual matter of becoming aware of some incongruity. If I notice an incongruity, but it distresses me in some way, then I am unlikely to laugh. Had I discovered a cobra in my refrigerator instead of the innocuous bowling ball mentioned earlier, my reaction would probably have been not to laugh but to slam the door and run. Similarly, seeing a young child full of life struck down by a car would be incongruous but not laugh-provoking. Fear, pity, moral disapprobation, indignation, or disgust, Beattie says, can override our tendency to laugh at incongruity. This is a point that will be developed later on.

To conclude, we cannot take it as universally true that laughter is a reaction to incongruity. Incongruity may well be involved in all humor, but is not involved in many cases of nonhumorous laughter. The incongruity theory, therefore, will not stand as a general theory of laughter.

# 4

# The Relief Theory

THE last theory I want to consider before turning to my own account of laughter is the relief theory. There are different versions of this theory, but they all have in common a more or less physiological point of view in which laughter is seen as a venting of nervous energy. While the superiority theory focuses on emotions involved in laughter, and the incongruity theory on objects or ideas causing laughter, the relief theory addresses a question little discussed in the other two theories, viz.: Why does laughter take the physical form it does, and what is its biological function?

One of the earliest places we find the relief theory hinted at is in Shaftesbury's essay of 1711, "The Freedom of Wit and Humour." "The natural free spirits of ingenious men, if imprisoned or controlled, will find out other ways of motion to relieve themselves in their constraint; and whether it be in burlesque, mimicry, or buffoonery, they will be glad at any rate to vent themselves, and be revenged on their constrainers."[1] Here we can see a possible overlap of the relief theory with a Hobbesian theory. To laugh in breaking free of constraint can also be to laugh in scorn at those who have been constraining one. In fact, one of the theorists who worked hardest at defending and developing the Hobbesian theory, Alexander Bain, was also one of the first to investigate psychological constraints and the role of laughter in breaking free of them.[2]

We can also combine the relief theory with the incongruity theory, if we look at our reason and the conceptual systems it builds as putting constraints on us. Schopenhauer, for example, speaks of laughter as involving an escape from the oppressive "Dame Reason." We could say, then, that the relief theory is not necessarily competing with the other two theories of laughter we have discussed; it is simply looking at a different aspect of the phenomenon. With this in mind, let us look at the role of relief in laughter.

There are two ways in which relief might fit into laughter situations. The person may have come into the situation with the nervous energy that is to be released, or the laughter situation itself may cause the build-up of the nervous energy, as well as its release. We can discuss these cases one at a time, starting with laughter and the release of pre-existing energy.

Any prohibition can cause a person to build up an increased desire to do what has been forbidden, and this frustrated desire may manifest itself in pent-up nervous energy. Children, for example, are often forced to sit still and be quiet when they are raring to run and shout. Their pent-up nervous energy shows in their overall muscle tension and in fidgeting. A more serious kind of pent-up energy would be found in those forced to live under the heavy restrictions of a dictatorship.

Many discussions of prohibitions leading to laughter cite traditional societal prohibitions against sex and violence. All cultures forbid some activities connected with sex. Many forbid intercourse outside of marriage, for example, and most have restrictions on when sex can even be talked about. Such restrictions cause people to suppress their sexual desires, according to the relief theory, and so when someone, say a comedian, breaks the taboo and talks about sex, forbidden sexual thoughts are called up and some of the sexual energy which has been repressed is released in laughter. Societal prohibitions on violence are supposed to cause a similar kind of repressed energy. If a schoolboy hates his teacher, for example, he is not allowed to take out his hatred by assaulting the teacher. Indeed, in repressing his hostile feelings he may even put on a show of respect and docility in the classroom. If the teacher should suffer violence at someone else's hand, however—say the student hears that the teacher was mugged—or if the teacher should simply trip and fall in front of the class, the pent-up energy of the student's hatred will find release in his laughter.

Freud thought that sex and hostility were the only drives whose repression led to laughter,[3] but in truth any taboo can set the stage for relief laughter. The Eighteenth Amendment made references to drinking alcohol funny in the United States. Antidrug laws have given comedians an easy way to get laughs among people who would like to see drug use uncontrolled—all they have to do is make allusions to using drugs. (As drug use has become more accepted in the last few years and as the legal penalties have been reduced, jokes about drug use have gotten progressively less response.)

The release in laughter, then, may be of nervous energy built up before the person entered the laughter situation. The other kind of release we mentioned is the release, not of pre-existing energy, but of energy built up by the laughter situation itself. When we listen to certain nonsexual, nonhostile jokes, for example, the narrative may arouse certain emotions in us toward the characters in the story. But then at the punch line the story takes an unexpected turn, or the characters are shown not to be what we thought they were, and so the emotional energy which has built up is suddenly superfluous and demands release. The release of this energy, according to the simplest version of the relief theory, is laughter.

Consider the following piece of doggerel by Harry Graham:

> I had written to Aunt Maud
> Who was on a trip abroad
> When I heard she'd died of cramp,
> Just too late to save the stamp.

The first three lines evoke in us feelings of sympathy for the poet, who has learned of the death of his aunt just after completing a letter to her. But the last line reveals that he is not at all the loving nephew we thought he was; his concern with the stamp shows that he was not bothered by his aunt's death, and so our sympathy for him is inappropriate. Oscar Wilde's quip, "The youth of today are quite monstrous; they have absolutely no respect for dyed hair," works in the same way. As we listen to it, all the way up to the second last word, we are led to feel the indignation of the adult generation against the younger generation. If the last two words had been "grey hair," then this feeling would have been appropriate, and our train of thought would have continued along the line that young people should revere the wisdom of their elders. But this train of thought is broken when we reach the words "dyed hair," for elders who dye their hair show that they do not have the wisdom capable of commanding the respect of the young. The emotion we have built up in listening to the earlier part of the quip is suddenly seen to be inappropriate, then, and is released in laughter.

In examining the relief theory of laughter I want to proceed by discussing first a relatively simple version of the theory, that of Herbert Spencer, and then the more complex theory of Freud. Spencer's theory is found in his essay "On the Physiology of Laughter."[4] There he says that our emotions are, or at least in our nervous system take the form of, nervous energy. And there is an intimate connection between nervous energy and our motor nervous system. "Nervous energy," he says, "always *tends* to beget muscular motion, and when it rises to a certain intensity, always does beget it."[5] It is a general law that "feeling passing a certain pitch habitually vents itself in bodily action."[6] In fear, for instance, we tend to make incipient movements of flight, and if the fear becomes great enough, we will flee the situation. When we are angry at a person, we tend to make small aggressive movements; we clench our fists, for example, and tighten our other muscles in preparation for action. And if the anger reaches a certain level we break into a physical attack on the person.

Laughter differs from the ordinary kinds of release of emotional energy, according to Spencer, in that the muscular movements in laughter are not the early stages of larger movements associated with some emotion. Clenching our fists and stomping our feet in anger work off some nervous energy, but if the anger increases these movements turn into the movements of physical attack. The muscular movements of laughter, however, do not lead to anything else. Laughter, even if intense, does not issue in any practical action. It does not take us out of a dangerous situation, it does not lead to fighting, etc. Indeed, some of the contemporary psychological literature suggests that laughter may serve to incapacitate the laugher, prevent him from, rather than prepare him for, doing anything.[7]

Laughing serves only to release nervous energy, Spencer says; other than that the bodily movements in laughter "have no object."[8]

The release of energy through laughter is accomplished, according to Spencer, when feelings are built up but then are seen to be inappropriate. The superfluous energy of those feelings is released first through the muscles "which feeling most habitually stimulates," viz., the muscles connected with speech.[9] If this channel of release is not adequate to handle all the nervous energy being discharged, then that energy will spill over into "less habitual" channels—the diaphragm and muscles associated with respiration will be stimulated to hearty laughter and then, if still more energy is to be released, the person may clap his hands, sway back and forth, etc.

Spencer's theory of laughter influenced many subsequent thinkers on the topic. John Dewey, for example, accounted for laughter as "the sudden relaxation of strain, so far as occurring through the medium of breathing and the vocal apparatus."[10] And Freud mentions Spencer by name, though he feels that Spencer's theory needs modifying. We will be considering Freud's version of the relief theory shortly, though before that we might offer some comments on the simpler and more general version of Spencer.

Clearly there is a connection between at least some laughter and the relief of tension or the expenditure of energy. We have all had the experience of being in danger, say of falling, and then laughing on regaining our security. The muscular tension of the dangerous state is relaxed as we regain our security. And all of us, presumably, after laughing very heartily, have felt that we have expended a great deal of energy, that in some way laughter has achieved a catharsis of nervous energy.

But it is a big step from observations like these to the claim that *all* laughter involves, or even *is*, the release of emotional nervous energy. One difficulty with this claim is that in many laughter situations, particularly humorous ones, there seems to be no emotional energy either brought into the situation, or developed within the situation, which "requires release." The laughter itself involves the expenditure of energy, of course, as any muscular movement does, but that is not energy which has somehow been "building up" within the person, and it need not be connected with feelings suddenly seen to be inappropriate. Consider, for example, Figure 1.

This cartoon can have its effect on us in a second or two, which is hardly long enough to arouse any emotion in us, much less to arouse some emotion and then to show it to be inappropriate. But then we must have brought some repressed emotion into our situation of viewing this cartoon, which that viewing allows us to release, if the relief theory is to apply to our appreciation of this cartoon. Yet it seems that we can enjoy this cartoon without releasing any repressed feelings at all. The cartoon is not sexual, and so, presumably, our laughter at it is not a release of repressed sexual feelings. And though it is conceivable that someone might laugh in scorn at the two characters portrayed here, and thus release repressed feelings of hostility toward optometrists or people in general, clearly we can laugh at this cartoon with no hostile feelings whatever pent up inside us. And the same seems true of lots of sight gags and jokes that work on similar kinds of incongruity.

If we look at nonhumorous cases of laughter, too, many of them seem to involve no pent-up emotions and no emotions toward whatever it is that makes us laugh. Laughing is unlike crying in this respect, I think, in that while we cannot cry without feeling some emotion toward the thing or situation making us cry, we can laugh without feeling emotion toward whatever it is making us laugh. Indeed, as I will try to show in developing my own account of laughter,

25

it is often possible to laugh only where we do *not* get emotionally involved with the laughter stimulus and do *not* have pent-up emotions.

Another problem with the relief theory is that its notion of feelings suddenly rendered superfluous does not seem to apply in certain cases where there is a build-up of emotion, because the conclusion of the stimulus is just what we were expecting and the feelings we had been building up are perfectly appropriate. Consider the hostile practical joke. If we are walking toward someone whom we dislike to offer him an exploding cigar, our excitement begins to build even before we reach him. And it increases as we offer him the cigar, he accepts, and we light it. When it explodes in his face, we laugh heartily, but not because the aggressive feelings which had been building up in us are suddenly rendered inappropriate. They were and still are perfectly appropriate to the situation—in a way, our laughter at the explosion of the cigar is the full expression of those feelings. This kind of situation is especially troublesome to Spencer's theory, in which the conclusion of a laughter stimulus must involve a "descending incongruity"; our emotions, he says, must change from strong emotion to weak emotion, so that the excess can be discharged in laughter. In cases like the exploding cigar, however, we have just the opposite: what starts as weak emotion gradually builds until it reaches its greatest strength at the moment of laughter.

Before moving on to consider Freud's more complex version of the relief theory, we should mention one last difficulty with Spencer's account. Laughing for Spencer is analogous to the opening of a safety valve in a steam pipe. Just as the opening of the valve releases excess steam pressure built up within the pipe, laughter is supposed to release excess nervous energy built up within the laugher's nervous system. But if this is the case, then we should expect the greatest amount of nervous energy to be released at the very beginning of the overflow, when the excess is at its peak. As the release continues, the amount of energy released, and so the intensity of the laughter, should gradually diminish; just as the steam released from a safety valve is at its greatest pressure at the moment the valve is opened, but after that initial outburst gradually diminishes. Now sometimes laughter is like this—there is a powerful outburst that trails off to mild chuckling and then no laughter at all. But often laughter starts out very weak and increases in strength; or there is an initial outburst followed by a period of no laughter, and then more laughter. If we explain laughter with a more mentalistic theory than Spencer's, as the expression of amusement, say, then we can account for such cases. As the person reacts to some laughter stimulus, he may at first be only mildly amused, but then as he thinks about it he becomes more amused. Or he may be amused, switch to thinking about something else for a moment, and then have thoughts of the laughter stimulus come back to make him laugh once more. But with a theory like Spencer's, which posits a fixed amount of surplus nervous energy to be released, it is hard to explain how there could be all this variation in the "overflow." The greatest intensity of stored nervous energy being released should come in the initial outburst, and then there should be a continuous decline in the strength of the laughter until all the surplus energy has been released. The fact that laughing does not always follow this pattern, and that often the laugher seems to "pick up steam" as he continues to laugh, shows us that Spencer's account is inadequate.

Let us turn, then, to another version of the relief theory, that of Freud. As is well known, Freud made a lot of the notion of psychic energy. And he was attracted by the way his friend Theodor Lipps and Spencer had worked the concept of psychic energy into a mechanical explanation of laughter. But Freud had to accommodate the relief theory to his general psychoanalytic theory, and this proved to be difficult.

Freud's basic work on the theory of laughter is found in his *Jokes and Their Relation to the Unconscious*.[11] In this book he distinguishes between three kinds of laughter situations, which he calls "jokes," "the comic," and "humor." The core of his theory is that in all laughter situations we save a certain quantity of psychic energy, energy that we have summoned for some psychic purpose but which turns out not to be needed, and this surplus energy is discharged in laughter. In joking, he says, we save energy that is normally used to suppress forbidden feelings and thoughts; in reacting to the comic we save an expenditure of energy in thought; and in humor we save an expenditure of energy in emotion.

Freud devotes most of his attention to jokes, and so, in examining his theory of laughter, we shall too. Let us start with Freud's views on the development of joking in the individual. At a certain stage, he says, children begin to play with words and ideas by juxtaposing them in a random way. Such play is not yet joking. As the child gets older, however, pressures are put on him to think logically and rationally, and this pressure extends even to his word and concept play. And so a second stage, which Freud calls "jesting," begins, in which the child puts words and ideas together in silly ways, but in ways that have some rational structure to them, just as adult jokes do. The third and final stage is true joking, in which the silliness of the jest is made to serve sexual or aggressive motives. Freud sometimes speaks of "innocent jokes" or "nontendentious jokes," but such phrases do not really belong in Freud's theory, as he sometimes reminds himself. "We must not forget that strictly speaking only jests are nontendentious."[12] If something is truly a joke and not merely a jest, then "it is either a *hostile* joke (serving the purpose of aggressiveness, satire, or defence) or an *obscene* joke (serving the purpose of exposure)."[13] The harmless playing with words and ideas found in children's jesting survives into adulthood, Freud thinks; he admits that there is such a thing as adult jesting. But he insists that our pleasure in jesting is of a different kind from our pleasure in joking, and is significantly less than the latter. Lacking the hostile or sexual purpose that a joke has, the jest works only on clever technique and not on content.[14]

We use jokes, Freud says, in order to let into our conscious minds forbidden thoughts and feelings, which our society has forced us to suppress. This is not a conscious process, for the suppressed thoughts and feelings originate in the unconscious. Joking, or at least the thinking up of jokes, is an involuntary process.[15] In this respect joking resembles dreaming, which is also a bringing out of suppressed thoughts and feelings from the unconscious.[16] Freud's claim here is doubtful at best, for at least some inventors of jokes—professional gag writers, for example—consciously and often systematically put jokes together. But we can overlook this point, for it is not crucial to our discussion.

More central as a difficulty in Freud's theory is his explanation of how jokes give us pleasure. The natural way for Freud to explain the pleasure of jokes would seem to be for him to say that it is pleasurable to release sexual or hostile feelings which one has been

28

suppressing, for this satisfies natural urges. And Freud does sometimes explain the pleasure of jokes in just this way. The hostile and sexual elements in jokes, he explains in one place, allow us to "evade restrictions and open sources of pleasure that have become inaccessible."[17] The pleasure in joking "arises from a purpose being satisfied whose satisfaction would otherwise not have taken place. That a satisfaction such as this is a source of pleasure calls for no further remark."[18] Had Freud left his account of the pleasure of laughter with these comments, his version of the relief theory would have been readily understandable, and would have been supported by some of the ordinary facts about laughter mentioned at the beginning of this chapter. But Freud's theory is greatly complicated by the fact that he gives another explanation of the pleasure of laughter, much less plausible than this simple one. The basic pleasure in laughter, he says, comes from a saving of psychic energy; laughter is the discharge of the saved energy. With this hypothesis Freud proposes to explain not just laughter at jokes, which he could already partially explain as the release of suppressed psychic energy, but also laughter at the comic, and laughter in humor, which could not be explained in that way. Because the saving of psychic energy operates differently in these three kinds of laughter, we should consider them one at a time.[19]

We can start with joking laughter. In our ordinary serious moments, Freud says, we use psychic energy to suppress our sexual and aggressive thoughts and feelings. But in joking we get to attend to these thoughts and express these feelings, rather than continuing to suppress them. The energy normally used for inhibition suddenly becomes superfluous, therefore—it is "saved"—and this energy is released in laughter. Notice here how Freud's account differs from the simpler account given by Spencer. In Spencer it is the energy of some emotion already aroused that is suddenly rendered superfluous, whereas in Freud it is the energy normally used to suppress the emotion that becomes superfluous. The pleasure of laughter in jokes, according to Freud, matches in intensity the effort it would have taken to suppress the feeling to which the joke gives release. "The hearer of the joke laughs with the quota of psychical energy which has become free through the lifting of the inhibitory cathexis; we might say that he laughs this quota off."[20]

The difference between Freud's theory and the simpler relief theory of Spencer might not at first seem to amount to much. After all, what is the difference between saying that the energy released in laughter is the energy of some built-up feeling, and saying that the energy released in laughter is the energy that has been summoned to suppress that feeling? But the problem with Freud is that it is hard to get a grasp on his notion of the energy of inhibition. The notion of psychic energy itself is problematic; certainly it is not well defined in Spencer. But we tend to let its vagueness go by in accounts like Spencer's, because we are able to think of some of our experiences of laughter in terms of the release of energy. We have all at some time experienced a relaxation after laughing, and so we have some idea of what Spencer is getting at when he says that laughter relieves the build-up of excess nervous energy. In Freud's account, however, not only is the notion of psychic energy vague, but the kind of psychic energy supposedly released in laughter is some new kind of energy, the energy of inhibition, about which we have few or no intuitions.

We have some idea of emotional energy building up and requiring release. There are times when we find it helpful to get outside and run, or punch a punching bag, for example, to "work off" our mounting anger at someone. The notion of releasing excess emotion, indeed, goes back at least as far as Aristotle's discussion of the catharsis of emotion in his *Poetics*. But the notion of a psychic energy used to inhibit feelings, which can be released when it is not needed, is not at all familiar. We do tell people "Try to control your emotions," but it is not at all clear that this commits us to the idea that there is a certain amount of psychic energy required for this control. The tension and uncomfortableness of containing one's emotions when they are very strong might simply be explained by saying that an urge is being frustrated; feelings calling for expression are not being expressed. If Freud wants to explain laughter in joking as the release of "saved" inhibitory energy, in short, he should first explain just what this kind of energy is and how we might measure, or at least detect, it. Until he does so, claims like the above that "the hearer of the joke laughs with the quota of psychical energy which has become free through the lifting of the inhibitory cathexis" will not have much explanatory value.

If the notion of inhibitory energy is problematic, so is Freud's notion of the saving and subsequent discharge of this energy. In

Spencer's theory, remember, emotional energy builds up to a certain level, the person suddenly realizes that that energy is unnecessary, and then it is released in laughter. The energy released, that is, is actual energy built up in the nervous system. But notice how different Freud's notion of an "economy of psychic expenditure" is. If I tell a joke about television repairmen as a way of expressing my hostility toward television repairmen, then in that situation I am not suppressing my hostile feelings toward television repairmen. We might even accept Freud's notion of inhibitory energy for the moment and say that there is a saving of the inhibitory energy I usually would have expended if the topic of television repairmen came up and I did not reveal my feelings toward them. But even if we go along with Freud this far, why would we say that the inhibitory energy I do not have to expend here is *actual energy* in the mind or nervous system, which is "left over" for discharge through laughter? To accept Freud's account here we would have to say that when we express a hostile feeling instead of suppressing it, we "summon" the energy to suppress it anyway. When someone mentions television repairmen, that is, I always generate the psychic energy required to suppress my hostile feelings toward them even if I am not going to suppress those feelings but instead express them in a joke I am about to tell. But all this sounds counterintuitive. It sounds much more plausible to simply say that when I am expressing my feelings, I neither suppress them nor summon the energy to suppress them. Even if we want to talk about the inhibitory energy that is saved, then, we should not think of it as actual energy in the mind or nervous system. Saved energy is not real energy that has to be discharged—it's simply energy that was never generated. Freud's reasoning here is mistaken in the same way as a sales pitch I heard once in a television commercial for a company that sold swimming pools: "And with all the money you save on the pool and filter, you'll be able to buy our deluxe diving board."

Before we turn to consider Freud's explanation of laughter at the comic and laughter at humor, we should mention one last difficulty with his account of jokes. Though key parts of his theory suffer from vagueness, as we have seen, the theory has certain general consequences. If Freud is right that the enjoyment of jokes comes from the release of energy used to suppress aggressive and sexual feelings, then we should be able to predict that the people who will enjoy aggressive jokes the most will be those who usually suppress their aggressive feelings, and that those who find sexual jokes the funniest will be those who usually suppress their sexual feelings.[21] But in the small amount of empirical research done in this area, these predictions have turned out to be wrong. Experiments by Eysenck have shown that people who generally express their sexual and aggressive feelings tend to enjoy sexual and hostile jokes more than those who generally suppress their feelings. "This means," Eysenck comments, "that a person's 'typical' behavior extends to his preferences in the humor field, instead of 'repressed' trends finding an escape through humor, as Freud had maintained."[22]

As we said earlier, Freud uses the notion of a saving of psychic energy to explain not just joking laughter but also his other two categories, comic laughter, and laughter at humor. We can consider these latter two categories one at a time.[23]

Our experience of the comic, Freud says, involves an economy of psychic energy in *thought*. In watching a circus clown stumble in his attempts at some simple task, for example, the economy is based on our comparison of the effort the clown is exerting to accomplish the task, with the much smaller effort we would exert to accomplish the same task. The comparison results in a saving of psychic energy, which then is released in laughter. The energy saved is not the energy that would be used to carry out the clown's movements or our own; it is the energy used to *understand* these movements. To understand a physical movement, or indeed anything at all, according to Freud, we go through a "mimetic representation" of the motion, object, or whatever, in our minds. And in this mental activity we expend psychic energy, a great amount to understand something big and a small amount to understand something small. Our mental representation of the clown's movements, then, calls for more psychic energy than our mental representation of what our own movements would be in the same situation, and the surplus energy here is released in laughter. "These two possibilities in my imagination amount to a comparison between the observed movement and my own. If the other person's movement is exaggerated and inexpedient, my increased expenditure in order to understand it is inhibited *in statu nascendi*, as it were in the act of being mobilized; it is declared superfluous and is free for use elsewhere or perhaps for discharge by laughter."[24]

Freud applies his "economy of psychic energy in thought" formula to other kinds of comic situations, but I don't think that we need go into them because his basic formula is so implausible. First of all, the principle that in understanding something big we expend great amounts of psychic energy, whereas in understanding something small we expend only a little energy has absurd consequences. Using it we would predict that astronomers, for example, must expend huge amounts of psychic energy, whereas watchmakers must expend almost none at all.

A second problem lies in explaining the mechanics of the discharge of the "surplus psychic energy" in laughter. According to Freud we use one small packet of psychic energy to understand how we might perform the task the clown is performing, and we use a larger packet of psychic energy to understand the clown's movements. And somehow as this latter packet of energy is being summoned, *in statu nascendi,* as Freud says, it is compared with the smaller packet and seen to be larger. But even if we were to follow Freud this far, it would not follow that the difference in psychic energy was somehow "superfluous" and available for discharge, as Freud claims. The energy he is talking about here, remember, is not energy that is going to be used to perform a physical movement (*that* kind of energy might conceivably be summoned and then be found unnecessary); this energy is psychic energy summoned to *understand* our own imagined movements and the movements of the clown. And though there is a difference in the amounts of psychic energy (following Freud for the moment), nothing is superfluous—the small packet is used in mentally representing the small movements we would make, and the large packet is used in mentally representing the large movements the clown is making. Here Freud might respond that we do not really "carry out" the understanding of the movements of the clown; the psychic energy is superfluous because it is not used for understanding the clown's movements. But if we do not in fact understand the clown's movements and what they are intended to accomplish, then it seems impossible to see how we could realize that they were extravagant. And how would we come to form any idea of what motions we might perform to accomplish the same task? If the psychic energy summoned to understand the clown's motions were not used to do just that, in short, the comparison Freud talks about would not occur.

Moreover, even if we ignore these problems and simply assent to Freud's claim that when the comic character expends more energy than we would, there is a saved energy of thought which is discharged in laughter, we face another difficulty. For there are many comic characters who make us laugh because they expend *less* energy, physically and mentally, than we would in the performance of some task. The comic-strip character Beetle Bailey, for example, is often funny just because he is so lazy and puts so little effort into whatever work he is doing. Freud tries to account for such cases by saying that in them there is still a difference between the energy the comic character expends and the energy we would expend, even though we would expend more, and that the comic effect depends only on the existence of this difference "and not on which of the two the difference favors."[25] But here Freud is changing the mechanics of his account significantly; if he wants to retain the notion that laughter is a discharge of superfluous energy, then he owes us an explanation of just what psychic energy is supposed to be superfluous.

And again, even if we let Freud get by with his expanded formula that we laugh because there is some difference between what the comic character does and what we would do, there are still comic cases not explained. Many comic situations involve a person trying to extricate himself from some predicament in just the ways any of us might, should we find ourselves in his shoes. The silent movies were full of such situations. When we watch Harold Lloyd get stuck out on a window ledge twenty stories above the pavement, and try various means of getting back inside, we can laugh even though he is neither extravagant nor lazy in his motions. Faced with such cases, Freud changes his account once more, and says that here we laugh because of a comparison, but not of the comic character with ourselves; we laugh because we compare the present state of the character to his former untroubled state.[26] But Freud's appeal to the difference here between the two states of the comic character will be plausible only if that difference somehow causes an excess of psychic energy in the person watching the comedy, an excess which is to be discharged in laughter. The same is true of Freud's extension of his "comparison" formula to cover comic incongruities in general:

> It is a necessary condition for generating the comic that we should be obliged, *simultaneously or in rapid succession,* to apply to one and the same act of ideation two different ideational methods, between which the "comparison" is then made and the comic difference emerges. Differences in expenditure of this kind arise between what belongs to someone else and to oneself, between what is usual and what has been changed, between what is expected and what happens.[27]

Judging by his comments on comedy of situation,[28] Freud would probably say that by empathizing with the character in the predicament we experience a small expenditure of psychic energy when he is in the safe situation, and then a large expenditure of psychic energy when he is in the predicament. But even if this is true, and even if we could show that all cases of comic laughter involved two expenditures of psychic energy of different quantities, it has not been explained where there is any superfluous energy in all this, which gets discharged in laughter. Unless Freud can offer such an explanation, I suggest, we should either reject his theory of comic laughter, or else take it, in its fully stretched-out form above, as a version of the incongruity theory, ignoring the references to psychic energy altogether.

Freud devotes only a few pages at the end of his book to his third category, laughter in humor, but it is here, perhaps, that his notion of a saving of psychic energy is applied most plausibly. Humor arises, Freud says, "if there is a situation in which, according to our usual habits, we should be tempted to release a distressing affect and if motives then operate upon us which suppress that affect *in statu nascendi.* . . The pleasure of humour . . . comes about . . . at the cost of a release of affect that does not occur: it arises from *an economy in the expenditure of affect.*"[29] As an example of humor, Freud cites Mark Twain's story of his brother who was working on building a road. An explosive charge went off prematurely and blew him into the sky, so that he landed far away from the work site. At this point in the story, Freud comments, we have summoned concern and pity for the poor man. But the end of Twain's story is that when his brother landed, he was docked half a day's pay for the time he was in the air "absent from his place of employment."[30] As we listen to this twist in the story, we realize that pity would be inappropriate here. "As a result of this understanding, the expenditure on the pity, which was already prepared, becomes unutilizable and we laugh it off."[31] Other pieces of humor operate with different emotions (Freud uses the term "emotion" in a broad way to cover not only pity and anger but also tenderness and piety), but in each case the emotion is summoned only to be seen as superfluous and hence suitable for discharge in laughter.

Perhaps one reason why Freud spent so little time sketching his theory of laughter at humor is that it is virtually a retelling of Spencer's account of laughter in general. As such, it requires no critical comments except what we have already said about Spencer's theory. Relief of tension or built-up emotional energy, as we saw, is sometimes part of laughter situations, but cannot be taken for the essence of laughter, since many laughter situations do not include it. Freud might respond here that laughter that does not involve the release of emotional energy is not troublesome for his theory, because, unlike Spencer, he does not purport to explain *all* laughter as the release of emotional energy, but only laughter at humor. This response, however, could only serve to defend Freud's theory of humor (not his theory of jokes and of the comic), if he could tell us what distinguishes humor from the comic and from jokes without simply saying that humor involves the release of emotional energy. That is, Freud cannot *define* humor in terms of a release of emotional energy in order to defend his theory that humor involves a release of emotional energy; if he did so, he would be left not with a theory of humor, but merely with the tautology that situations involving the release of emotional energy involve the release of emotional energy.

If we had workable characterizations of Freud's other two categories of laughter—joking laughter and laughter at the comic—we might be able to figure out by a process of elimination what humor is for Freud, and then inquire whether all cases of humor do involve a release of emotional energy. But we do not have such workable characterizations, for, as with humor, Freud tries to distinguish joking laughter and laughter at the comic in terms of which kind of psychic energy is released in each of them. And as we have seen, we have good reasons for doubting the *existence* of a release of inhibitory energy (his definition of joking laughter), and of a release of energy resulting from a comparison in thought.

Freud's complex relief theory, to conclude, is plausible only where the simpler relief theory is plausible, and that is in pointing out that laughter situations *sometimes* involve a release of nervous energy. Since the simple relief theory cannot stand as a comprehensive theory of laughter, however, neither can Freud's theory.

# 5

# A New Theory

It would be possible, of course, to examine many other versions of the three theories of laughter we have considered, as well as theories such as Bergson's which add new elements to one of them or to a combination of them. But for our purposes this is unnecessary. In each case our basic conclusion would be the same—that no version of any of these theories is comprehensive enough to account for all cases of laughter.

We have not been wasting our time in examining the superiority theory, the incongruity theory, and the relief theory, however, for each has drawn our attention to an important aspect of laughter, which a comprehensive theory will have to account for. A comparison of these theories, in fact, suggests three general features of laughter situations that can form the basis of a comprehensive theory. The first feature is the change of psychological state that the laugher undergoes. This change may be primarily cognitive, as the incongruity theory shows—from a serious state of perceiving and thinking about things that fit into our conceptual patterns, to a nonserious state of being amused by some incongruity. The change may be primarily affective, as in cases described by superiority and relief theories, in which laughter accompanies a boost in positive feelings, a cessation of negative feelings, or the release of suppressed feelings.

Or the change may be both cognitive and affective, as in cases of hostile humor.

Not just any change in psychological state will trigger laughter, however. As the three theories we have looked at show, the change must be sudden. To laugh, we must be caught off guard by the change so that we cannot smoothly adjust to what we are experiencing. This second feature of laughter situations will require more discussion later, but for now we can build it into our notion of a psychological change by henceforth talking not about psychological changes, but about psychological "shifts," which we will understand to be *sudden* changes.

And the third feature which must be added to our characterization of laughter situations is that the psychological shift is pleasant. Enjoying self-glory, being amused by some incongruity, releasing pent-up energy—all these feel good, and can cause us to laugh. An unpleasant psychological shift, on the other hand, such as learning of the death of a loved one, or being confronted with some distressing incongruity, is not the kind of thing that makes us laugh. (At the end of this chapter we will consider laughter in embarrassment and hysteria, which are only apparent counterexamples.) Now we can put these three features together into a formula for characterizing laughter situations in general:

*Laughter Results from a Pleasant Psychological Shift*

I say "results from" here because laughter is neither the psychological shift itself nor the pleasant feeling produced by the shift. Laughter is rather the physical activity which is caused by, and which expresses the feeling produced by, the shift. The feeling itself we might call "amusement" or "mirth," though as Beattie and others have noted, we have no single, agreed-upon word to designate the feeling expressed in laughter. And the lack of a word here is not merely linguistically troublesome, for it has caused at least some theorists not to distinguish clearly enough between laughter as a physical behavior, and the feeling—amusement, I will call it—which laughter expresses.

The formula just given is very general, but we should expect a comprehensive theory of laughter to be very general; as we have seen, narrower formulas are able to account for only some cases of laughter. Generality would be a problem here only if it made the theory vacuous as applied to specific cases of laughter. But, as I will try to show, this is not the case. To see how this theory covers the many kinds of laughter listed in Chapter 1, and does so in an illuminating way, then, let us look at the development of laughter.

We can start with the simplest cases of nonhumorous laughter in the infant. In its earliest months the infant's world is very different from our own. Its simple psychology involves sensory stimulation through skin, eyes, ears, etc., but does not yet include perception of objects. The infant does not identify objects nor even distinguish between its own body and what is not its body. When the young infant begins to laugh at three or four months, therefore, the psychological shift prompting the laughter is not conceptual nor even perceptual; it is merely a shift in sensory input.

The simplest kind of laughter stimulus in the young infant is tickling. In being tickled the baby alternately feels stimulation in its skin and underlying tissues, and does not feel stimulation. If the touching or poking were constant instead of intermittent, the infant would probably feel it as painful or at least as uncomfortable. But in tickling, as soon as the stimulation starts, it stops, only to begin again, and so on. If the timing of the touches is right, if a familiar voice accompanies them, and if nothing else is bothering the infant at the time, this shift in sensory input will be pleasant to it, and its laughter is the expression of its pleasure.

Older children and adults, of course, can also be tickled; and though more is involved here because a child or adult perceives the tickler, and can often thereby anticipate or even stop the touches, here, too, successful tickling is based on a shift in sensory stimulation. The most important thing in tickling children and adults is that the touch be unexpected in some way—either in its commencement, duration, location, direction, or amount of pressure. For if we can fully anticipate the touch, we can prepare ourselves for it and so eliminate its suddenness, its power to shock us; in that case there will not be a psychological shift, but merely an expected bit of stimulation. This is why, as Aristotle explained, a person cannot tickle himself; the laugh of tickling, he said, comes from "a sort of surprise and deception" which is not possible with oneself.[1] Léon Dumont extended these observations. If you tell someone that you are going to touch him at a certain spot and then do so, he will not laugh. But if you make a movement as if to pinch him and then do not touch him, he will laugh. If you pass your fingers over the person's skin without varying the speed or direction, moreover, or if you touch him at completely regular intervals, you will not achieve the effect of tickling him.[2]

A full treatment of tickling in children and adults would take into account other perceptual and conceptual factors, such as the person's relationship to the tickler; it would even have to discuss the humor that is found in some tickling of children and adults. But that would take us too far ahead of ourselves—let us return to the simpler cases of nonhumorous laughter in babies. If we look at the kinds of nonhumorous laughter listed in Chapter 1, we find one other type of laughter in babies that is based on a shift in sensory stimulation: the laugh at being tossed into the air and caught. As the baby is tossed upwards, it feels movement and the lack of support. In contrast with the kinaesthetic feelings experienced in simply being held, these feelings are exhilarating, though if they continue for long or increase in intensity, the baby might feel discomfort. But before these feelings become uncomfortable, the baby is caught and the feelings of the secure rest state return. And then it is tossed and caught once more. If conditions are right, so that the shift in feelings doesn't distress the baby, it will experience the shift as pleasurable and laugh. The adult counterpart to this kind of laughter is laughing on a roller-coaster ride.

When the baby gets to the stage where it not only has sensory input, but can perceive objects, then it is capable of a more sophisticated kind of psychological shift. The baby who picks out objects in its visual experience will laugh, for example, at the game of peekaboo. For older children and adults peekaboo does not usually cause laughter because, though it involves a change in what is perceived, that change is a relatively small one—it is simply the alternate covering and uncovering of someone's face. What makes this change too small to cause amusement is our knowledge that the other person is right there all along whether we can see him or not. At the stage where babies enjoy peekaboo, however, they have not yet learned

41

about the constancy of objects—that they continue to exist even when they are not seen. As Piaget has shown, before babies are about eight months old, they do not understand that objects can disappear from view and yet still continue to exist; this is why they will not search for an object that is taken away from them and placed behind or under something else.[3] For these young Berkeleyans *esse est percipi*. And so peekaboo involves not a minor but a major change in their perceptual field—it is not the alternate covering and uncovering of the face, but the alternate existence and nonexistence of the face. Analogous to the baby's laughter at the perceptual shift in peekaboo is the adult's laughter at a magic trick in which an object, especially a large object, is made to suddenly appear or disappear.

Now these sensory and perceptual shifts we have been discussing amuse babies and cause them to laugh, but they do not constitute humor. For there to be humor a more sophisticated kind of psychological shift is required—a conceptual shift. By the age of three or four children are able to identify objects and know that they exist independently of their perceiving them. But more importantly, they have developed a set of concepts for understanding the things, properties, and events in their experience. They distinguish between *people* and *animals*, for example, and know that red, green, and blue are all the same kind of property—they are all *colors*. Most children, of course, acquire these and other concepts in acquiring language. Indeed, a common way of explaining what concepts are is to say that they are the meanings of our words.

But the child does more than just acquire a group of labels for naming things, properties, and events in his experience; he also comes to see certain patterns among them. Fire, for example, is always hot. When he sees fire, therefore, he expects it to be hot. Similarly, he will come to associate certain expressions on his parents' faces, and certain tones in their voices, with anger, approval, etc. The child develops not just a set of concepts, in short, but a whole system of connections between them. This conceptual system, or picture of the world, as we might call it, is based on the child's past experience, and serves as the basis of his expectations for what his future experience will be like.

Once the child has developed such a picture of the world, and has operated with it for awhile, he can begin to enjoy humor. In the beginning, of course, the conceptual shifts in the child's humor will be very simple. Most adult humor, at least in our culture, is based on experiencing or imagining incongruity—some thing or situation with features that are somehow inappropriate—but children often find something humorous simply because they have not experienced anything like it before. The conceptual shift in adult humor is usually from what the person would expect a given thing or situation to be like, to an awareness that the thing or situation is not like that, that it has incongruous features. The person has experienced things or situations of this kind before, but not with these unusual features. The surprise here is based on having part of one's conceptual system violated. But in the simplest kind of children's humor, the shift is more elementary than this. It is from an ordinary state of awareness in which the child understands the things and events he is experiencing, to a surprised state of confronting some new *kind* of thing or event for which he has not prepared a place in his picture of the world. His conceptual system has not been violated by something incongruous; since he is experiencing a new kind of thing, he has no expectations about what features it should have.

This simple kind of laughter at what is brand new often occurs, for example, on the child's first visit to the zoo. When an adult sees an animal he hasn't seen before, he is likely—because he thinks with the general categories "animal," "mammal," "bird," etc.—to assimilate that experience to his past experience of animals, mammals, birds, etc. Because he has these general concepts, no animal will seem completely new to him. But the child's concept of "animal" will be much more limited—it may include, say, only dogs and cats. And so when he sees something like an ostrich for the first time, it is likely that he has no place at all for it in his conceptual system. For him it will be a brand-new kind of thing, and seeing it will shift him from an ordinary state of awareness to one of astonishment. If this shift is pleasant to him, and not, say, threatening, he will laugh.

This laughter at experiencing new kinds of things, of course, becomes less frequent as the child grows up and gains familiarity with more of the kinds of things there are. By the time we are adults, most of us have conceptual systems that are relatively adequate to handle the things and events we will run across. To find adult examples of the simple kind of laughter we have been discussing, the best place to look is probably at situations in which so-called primitive peoples are exposed to Western technology and customs for the first time; here adults are in a position similar to that of our own children in facing new *kinds* of things. An early record of how the natives of Borneo reacted to Western ways, for example, tells how a group of these people were greatly amused the first time they saw a piano played with its inner workings visible. The movement of the hammers and the dampers was something the likes of which they had not experienced before, and they laughed heartily.[4] A similar story is told of the natives of Fiji, who, because they are in the water so much, never have to wash themselves; when they first saw Europeans washing their faces, they were utterly astounded and laughed a great deal.[5]

Having discussed the laugh of simple surprise, then, we can turn to the other, more advanced kind of humor, in which what is funny to the person is not something totally unfamiliar to him, but something incongruous according to his conceptual system. When someone puts on a dog's head from a costume to amuse the four-year-old, for example, the child laughs not because this dog/human is totally unfamiliar; for he has experienced both dogs and people before. What amuses him is the incongruity here, the violation of his conceptual system in which a dog is one thing and a person is another. Or if the young child puts together incompatible ideas by himself, as in saying something like "Daddy baby" while experimenting with his newly acquired language, what gives him an enjoyable jolt is not the individual ideas here, but their absurd juxtaposition.

It is precisely because humor involves a tinkering with the child's very conceptual system, his picture of the world, that it takes children a while to catch on to humor. Just when they are getting the hang of adults talking to them to convey information, ask questions, give commands, etc., they are confronted with an adult who says something like, "I'm going to eat you up," or who asks, "Are you a *doggy*?" For some children early experiences with the conceptual shifts that are supposed to be amusing are instead puzzling or even distressing. The child cannot enjoy humor, or even experience it as humor, until he catches on to the fact that the incongruities he is being presented with are only a playful rearranging of reality and not, say, a confusing bunch of preposterous lies. Before the child can play around with his conceptual system, in short, he has to have a pretty solid grasp of that system, and has to feel comfortable in having it violated.

The development of humor does not stop, of course, when the child is able to enjoy simple incongruities; his capacity for humor will increase and grow in sophistication as he develops intellectually and emotionally. For the first few years, humor will consist mostly of simple incongruities based on the child's strongly perceptual orientation. Seeing someone dressed in inappropriate clothes, or calling something by the wrong name (especially calling a boy a girl or vice versa) will be major sources of amusement. Then, around the age of six, as the child's reasoning becomes more abstract and more logical, he develops a liking for joking riddles such as the "moron" riddles. ("Why did the moron throw the clock out the window?" "Because he wanted to see time fly.") After the age of eight, riddles start giving way to funny stories with punch lines, until at about age twelve joking stories predominate in children's humor. As the child gets older, too, the way the joke is told becomes important. Cleverness, style, and especially brevity, which don't matter among six-year-olds, can make the difference between a joke's getting and not getting a laugh among twelve-year-olds. During the adolescent years increasingly sophisticated kinds of humor are appreciated; real-life anecdotes told in a funny way, and wit, come into prominence.[6]

In Chapter 6 we will discuss the conceptual shift in different kinds of humor; and so we need not detail here how our formula that laughter results from a pleasant psychological shift applies to each of the cases of humorous laughter on the list in Chapter 1. But our stress so far on sensory and cognitive shifts leading to laughter needs to be supplemented by a discussion of emotional shifts, for without an understanding of the latter we cannot understand most of the cases of nonhumorous laughter on our list, or the cases, such as hostile humor, in which a conceptual shift is accompanied by an emotional shift.

We might begin our examination of emotional shifts by looking at a relatively simple case of nonhumorous laughter, laughing on regaining one's safety after being in danger. There is a cognitive dimension, of course, to this experience, as there is in emotions generally. The person at first recognizes that he is about to fall, say, and then on regaining his balance recognizes that he is no longer in danger. But what leads to the laughter here is the emotional change between these two states of fearful tension and relaxed security. Emotions are based on perceptions; but here it is the emotional shift that is experienced as pleasurable and leads to the laughter. If the object about to fall were something about which he did not care, say a scrap of paper about to blow off a table, then the mere knowledge that something was about to fall but did not would not be enough to make him laugh (unless he found that situation somehow incongruous and therefore humorous).

A similar kind of emotional shift is behind a person's laughing on solving a puzzle or problem. If the solution comes in a straightforward way, with relatively little effort, then the person will not laugh. But if he experiences tension and frustration because the solution does not come easily, then he will probably experience an emotional shift when he does find the solution. At one moment he will be focusing all his attention and effort on the puzzle, and feeling frustrated and annoyed that he has not found the solution; and at the next moment he will have the solution, and so feel an end to his frustration and annoyance. This emotional shift feels pleasurable, and so he laughs. Winning an athletic contest or game can cause laughter in a similar way, if the contest or game has been a real struggle for the person.

The shift that causes laughter, moreover, need not be from a negative emotional state to a positive one. It may be from a nonemotional state to a positive emotional state. In the situation where I run into an old friend on the street, for instance, I may be experiencing no emotion before I see him. But then as I recognize his face and rush to meet him, I feel a boost of excitement; my step quickens and even my heartbeat is speeded up. The shift from feeling no emotions to feeling very strong emotions here will be pleasant, and my hearty laughter will be the expression of my pleasure. In much the same way I might laugh on finding out that I have won a lottery, especially if this discovery is accidental and so sudden. Even the shift from a neutral emotional state to simply *thinking* about something that arouses positive emotions can be enough to trigger laughter, as when we laugh in anticipating some enjoyable activity or in recalling some particularly fond memory.

46

Hobbes was on the right track, then, in recognizing that a sudden boost in positive emotion can cause laughter (though he was wrong that the emotion need be self-focused). And the relief theory is correct that a laughter situation can involve a sudden change from a tense state to a relaxed state, a "release of emotional energy," if you will. The mistake in these theories lies in their attempt to explain all cases of laughter as being essentially the same as these limited cases. As we have seen, the psychological shift leading to laughter may be an emotional shift, but it need not be; it may be simply a sensory, a perceptual, or a conceptual shift.

So far, we have been distinguishing nonhumorous laughter at different kinds of emotional shifts from humorous laughter at a conceptual shift. But we should point out that in many cases of humorous laughter, the enjoyment of a conceptual shift is accompanied by and boosted by the enjoyment of an emotional shift. If I am watching a movie in which someone at a gambling casino accidentally falls against a slot machine, pulls down the arm of the machine in breaking his fall, and thereby hits the jackpot, I might laugh at the incongruity of this turn of events. But if I were in a casino myself and the same thing happened to me, my enjoyment of the incongruity would be accompanied by my enjoyment of my sudden good fortune. Similarly, if in a comedy someone accidentally falls into a swimming pool fully clothed, I may enjoy the incongruity of this event. But if I dislike my neighbor for the way he flaunts his wealth, then when I see him fall into his swimming pool in his new $500 suit, I will laugh not only because I enjoy the incongruity here, but also because of the sudden feeling of delight I experience at the setback of this person I dislike.

We should not put too much emphasis on the emotional shift present in some cases of humor, however, as Freud's theory and others have done, for our enjoyment of an emotional shift is neither necessary nor sufficient for humor, whereas our enjoyment of a conceptual shift is both necessary and sufficient for humor. Though a release of hostile, sexual, or other feelings may be involved in some cases of humor, the essence of humor lies in the enjoyment of incongruity.

Let us return, then, to our discussion of the emotional shift in nonhumorous kinds of laughter. Looking back at our list of nonhumorous laughter situations in Chapter 1, we have been able to account for all but the last three with our formula that laughter is a reaction to a pleasant psychological shift. These last three—laughing out of embarrassment, hysterical laughter, and laughing under the influence of nitrous oxide—are not as easy to explain. But before discussing them, I want to examine in more detail two elements in our formula, the suddenness of the psychological change and the pleasure involved. By understanding these elements better we will be better equipped to understand the three cases above, and laughter generally.

Let us start with suddenness, the notion that we capture by using the term "shift" to talk about the psychological change in laughter. Ordinarily the word "sudden" can mean either "unexpected" or "fast," though in the notion of a sudden psychological change, these amount to the same thing. For a sudden psychological change is one that we cannot assimilate into our experience in the way we can assimilate other psychological changes. It happens too fast for us to adjust to what is happening. An unexpected change of sufficient magnitude will be sudden in this sense.

Where a change is expected, where we know in advance that it is about to occur, then we can adjust ourselves for that change. We will be prepared to assimilate that change relatively smoothly (if it is not *too* great), because we will begin to react psychologically to the change before it occurs. To take an example of a sensory change, if someone is pushed without warning into a swimming pool filled with fairly cool water, he will experience much more of a psychological shift than if he has decided to jump into the pool, braced himself for the cool temperature of the water, and then jumped in.

We can see the necessity of suddenness in the laughter situations we have considered. A person cannot tickle himself, as was mentioned, even though his fingers might do exactly what someone else's fingers would do in tickling him; because he will know what's coming and so, no matter how fast he may poke his own ribs, the psychological change will not be fast. And in peekaboo, if instead of covering and uncovering our face quickly, we were to do so very slowly, so that the change in the baby's perceptual field were gradual, the baby would not laugh. Or if we repeat the covering and uncovering too often, or at too regular intervals, so that the baby

48

gets used to what is happening, then the baby's psychological changes will no longer be sudden, and he will stop laughing.

This is not to say that only a sudden change can be experienced as *pleasant*—only that a change which is not sudden will not produce *laughter*. We can bring out the difference between a pleasant change that does not produce laughter and one that does, with another example of a temperature change. If someone gets into a tub of lukewarm water and slowly mixes in hot water until the whole tub is hot (but still comfortable), he would probably enjoy the change in temperature he experiences. But unless some other factor were involved, such a slow gradual change would not cause him to laugh. If, instead, someone has already filled the tub with hot water and, not knowing what temperature it is, he plunges himself into it, the temperature change he experiences may also be pleasant; but here it will be pleasant *and* sudden. The change in temperature will "hit" him, as we say, it will occur faster than he can smoothly adjust to it. And so, if the change is pleasant, he may well laugh.

Suddenness in a psychological change, then, is a function of the amount of change (the difference between the earlier state and the later) and the time over which the change takes place. For a sudden change there must be a relatively large difference between the two states, and the time separating these states must be relatively short. If the time is short but the change is small, then the change is not sudden, for the person can assimilate what is happening. And if the change is great but the time is also great, here too the rate of change is slow, the person can adjust smoothly to what is happening, and there is no "jolt." Knowing in advance that a certain change is about to take place, as we said, has the same effect in reducing suddenness as spreading the change over more time, for the person who is expecting a certain change has already started to adjust to it.

The need for suddenness in the psychological change is perhaps even more evident in humorous laughter than in nonhumorous laughter. Indeed, this element of suddenness is built into much of our talk about humor. We speak of a joke's "hitting" us, and the conclusion of a joke as its "punch line." A successful comedian is said to have "knocked them out" or "slain them." And a piece of humor that does not "hit" us is said to be "weak."

A weak joke may fail because the incongruity in the joke is too small. Or the incongruity may be too familiar to us from hearing similar jokes before; this really amounts to the same thing, since the more familiarity we gain with an incongruity the less incongruous it becomes. In either case we are able to process the punch line conceptually with relative smoothness. A joke may fail, too, even if it is based on a large and unfamiliar incongruity, if it fills in too many of our conceptual steps for us. Some joke tellers, for example, try to make sure that no one can miss the point of their joke, by introducing the incongruity in very small, thoroughly explained steps. But by doing this they sabotage their own joke, for an incongruity fully prepared for and thoroughly explained is no longer an incongruity. The punch line of such a joke will be processed by our understanding with relative ease, no conceptual shift will take place, and so there will be no laughter. This is also, of course, why explaining a joke to someone who does not get it will almost never make him laugh.

The need for suddenness also accounts for the fact that most pieces of humor will have their full effect on us only once. In listening to a joke for the second time, the punch line can no longer catch us off guard, at least to the same extent it did the first time. And by the third or fourth time we hear it, it is unlikely that we will laugh at all, except perhaps to feign amusement for the benefit of the person telling the joke. This is not to deny that there are certain classic pieces of humor that maintain a good share of their freshness even with numerous repetitions. I have watched some of the old "Honeymooners" sketches on television four or five times, for example, and have laughed each time. In one sketch Ralph (Jackie Gleason) and Norton (Art Carney) are trying to get an obstruction out of the hose on a vacuum cleaner. Ralph puts his mouth to the end of the hose and tries to blow it out; meanwhile Norton, not paying attention, decides to turn the machine on to suck it out. I laugh at this scene each time, in part, because it is so rich in comic details. The first time I saw it I focused primarily on the expression on Gleason's face as the vacuum hose between his lips begins to suck all the air out of his mouth. But on subsequent viewings I noticed lots of equally funny details in the sketch—the way Ralph tries to signal Norton with his hand to shut the motor off, Norton's scrambling when he does try to turn it off, etc. Because of this richness of incongruity, I have not gotten fully adjusted to seeing this scene even after the fifth time, and so it maintains a good deal of its power to surprise and delight me.

There is an interesting connection here between what we find humorous or funny, and what we find to be fun. What makes an activity fun is not just that it is pleasant (eating familiar food is often pleasant yet not fun), but that it has an element of surprise for us. Children have a great capacity for having fun doing even simple things, because so much of the world is unfamiliar to them. Adults often play games to have fun; and a game with lots of turns of action is more fun—even for the eventual winner—than one in which it is clear from the start who is going to win. Activities stop being fun for us when there are no longer any surprises, when they have become so familiar to us that what happens next is predictable. Many people have the most fun doing something like skiing or sailing before they get really good at it; complete mastery of a skill, paradoxically, can take a good share of the fun out of it.

The place of suddenness in humor also explains another interesting phenomenon—that very often the creator of humor does not laugh himself. The person who makes the wisecrack that gets everyone else laughing, for example, may well have no trouble keeping a straight face. And the writer of a comedy may well experience no particular amusement in putting together the hilarious events in his play. What makes such cases possible is that creators of humor often construct their witty comments or incongruous situations out of elements with which they are familiar and in patterns which they have used often, in much the same way as a painter sets up a design or works out a color scheme for one of his canvases. When the witty statement is uttered, or the scene in the comedy is acted on the stage, of course, the audience will be caught off guard and so will laugh. But for the creator of the humor, there may have been no suddenness to the way the ideas were put together; he is not caught off guard by the incongruity, because he constructed it. This is not always the case, to be sure. A humorist may sometimes have a funny idea come to him with just as much suddenness as it will then be presented to his audience. And in these cases he may laugh just as hard as they will.

Having discussed the first element in our formula, suddenness, then, we can turn now to the second element, which is the pleasure in laughter. We see the connection between laughter and pleasure in the earliest laughter of the infant on being tickled. If the tickling goes on too long, or becomes too intense, so that it stops being pleasant, the baby will stop laughing and begin to cry. Or in the game of peekaboo, if the mother's face is covered for too long a time so that the baby starts to feel abandoned, laughter will likewise give way to tears.

Laughter in older children and adults is more complicated; for though it is still the natural expression of pleasure at a psychological shift, as it was in the baby, it is no longer merely an involuntary response to a stimulus. Now it is also a piece of learned behavior, at least partially under the person's control. Like crying, laughter can now be suppressed when it is the natural response to a particular stimulus. And it can be performed as an action under various circumstances where the person is not feeling pleasure, the laugh of embarrassment being a paradigm case. I want to leave aside such problem cases for the moment, however, and examine laughter as the natural expression of pleasure at a psychological shift. Having done that, we will be able to return to explain such phenomena as the laugh of embarrassment.

In the standard cases, then, the psychological shift that triggers laughter is pleasant. Finding out that one has won a lottery, for instance, might cause such a shift and make the person laugh. Discovering that a friend had been killed, on the other hand, though it may involve just as big a psychological shift, would not produce laughter because it is not pleasant. Similarly, watching someone fall out of an airplane in a slapstick movie might strike us as funny, but the same incident in real life, because it would evoke negative emotions, would not. As we saw in examining Beattie's incongruity theory, a psychological shift can be unpleasant if it evokes any of a number of negative emotions: fear, pity, indignation, disgust, etc.

Often the difference between a pleasant and an unpleasant shift, one which leads to laughter and one which does not, is relatively small. If I am in an average mood when I make a blunder like pouring coffee on my breakfast cereal, I will usually enjoy the situation and laugh; but if I am slightly out of sorts, my reaction may be one of frustration or even anger. Similarly, if I see you bump your head lightly on a door, I may laugh, especially if the expression on your face indicates that you are not hurt. But if the bump is a little harder so that your pain is significant, I probably will not laugh but instead feel sympathy for you.

A psychological shift, furthermore, does not have to evoke negative emotions like anger and pity in order to block laughter. If it evokes an attitude of puzzlement, wonder, curiosity, or problem solving, the person may not laugh. Young children, for example, sometimes react to a supposedly humorous incongruity with one of these attitudes and so do not laugh. On seeing an adult with an animal mask over his head, the child may simply stand there confused. Or his curiosity may be aroused—he may approach the person to get a closer look, try to touch the mask, etc. In either case he does not take the incongruity as humorous and simply enjoy it, but instead takes it as some kind of cognitive challenge. Like the adult at the magic show who spends all his time trying to figure out how the previous trick was done, his attitude is one of "reality assimilation," as Paul McGhee calls it.[7]

In order to enjoy a psychological shift, too, as indeed to enjoy any experience, we need to be without urgent practical needs. The shift itself cannot necessitate some action on our part to avoid injury or stay alive, say, and our overall state at the time must be relatively secure. What Ralph Piddington says of "biologically determined laughter" can be applied to laughter generally: the mood of laughter is one "in which there is no need felt for the organism to make any further adjustment to its environment".[8] Though this element of security is usually present in laughter situations both before and after the shift occurs, we should note, it need not always be present before the shift; for as we have seen, the shift may itself be from a state of practical concern and negative emotion to one of safety.

A helpful way to understand the connection between laughter and security is to contrast laughing with crying as a reaction to an event with undesirable practical consequences.[9] When such an event occurs, and causes a psychological shift in us, we tend to laugh if we still feel secure and in control of the situation; we tend to cry, on the other hand, if the psychological shift has made us feel insecure and not in control. We might feel still in control of the situation, for example, if the negative consequences are trivial, as when I poured the coffee on my breakfast cereal. Or if the matter is not trivial, as when we make blunders that will cost time and money to correct, we may still feel in control if we can adjust our viewpoint to "rise above" the practical side of the situation (more on this later when we talk about humor and "distancing"). When people cry, by contrast, it is because what has happened is not trivial to them and cannot be "risen above." Instead, the psychological shift they have experienced has made them feel helpless. Crying is the expression not just of *displeasure* at some turn of events (many events displease us but don't make us cry), but of *distress,* displeasure plus a feeling of powerlessness.

Studies with both children and adults have shown the connection of laughter with the person's sense of security and control. People who have a positive self-concept and a confident view of themselves as masters of their own fate laugh and enjoy humor more than those who do not feel in control. Those who are least in control, and who cry the most, of course, are babies. Since they can do nothing for themselves for a long time, whatever security they feel comes from the way others treat them. Crucial here is the child's being touched and held. Infants who are not given this "mothering" feel even more helpless, and cry more than other infants; indeed they often cry at the same stimulus which makes more secure "mothered" infants laugh.[10]

In raising children we encourage them to develop control over their environment, to walk, to talk, to feed themselves, etc. And if they cry in inappropriate situations, or in appropriate situations but for too long, we try to get them to stop crying and take control of the situation. We may assure them that what has happened is relatively trivial and does not affect their overall well-being; or, as when children have failed at something important, we encourage them that they are still in control—it just takes more effort or practice. "Don't be a crybaby, try again," we tell them.

We often try to get children, and adults too, to regain their feeling of security and stop crying, by making them laugh. All our talk about laughter as the *product* of a feeling of security, and as the expression of pleasure, should not mislead us into thinking that there is only a one-way causal relation here. Laughing, like crying, is not a mere epiphenomenon of some completely nonbehavioral internal feeling. William James was extreme, I think, in saying that a man does not cry because he is sad, but is sad because he cries. And yet this comment is helpful in steering us away from thinking that our behavior does not affect our feelings. The truth is that there is two-way causality between our feelings and the behavior expressing those feelings. If we can change a person's behavior from crying to laughing, to some extent we thereby change his feelings and make him less upset by his situation. Indeed, even with those diseases such as multiple sclerosis, in which occasional bouts of pathological laughter are triggered completely physiologically, patients report that they feel good after this laughter, even though it was not originally caused by a pleasant feeling.[11] There is a causal loop here. Laughing is a behavior that expresses pleasant feelings. But this behavior is itself pleasant, and so tends to increase pleasant feelings. It is possible, then, to break into the loop by starting with just the laughter (performed voluntarily or caused physiologically), which will induce pleasant feelings, which feelings may in turn cause more laughter.

With this understanding of the relation of laughter to the pleasure it expresses, and the place of feelings of security and control in this pleasure, we can now return to explain two of our problem cases—the laugh of embarrassment and laughter in hysteria. After that, we can say something about our last problem case, laughter under the influence of nitrous oxide.

Embarrassment and hysteria, to begin, seem unlikely situations in which to expect laughter if our theory is correct that laughter is an expression of pleasure at a psychological shift; for though we may grant that there is a psychological shift in these cases, it seems clearly an unpleasant rather than a pleasant one. In embarrassment we suddenly feel self-conscious and uncomfortable in front of others, usually because of something wrong or silly that we've done. And the laugh of hysteria typically occurs in a situation where a person discovers something shocking, such as the death of a loved one. What is felt in these cases is not security, control, and pleasure, but rather distress.

To understand how laughter in embarrassment and hysteria do fit into our account, we can compare them to the case above in which we try to get the crying person to feel less upset in a distressing situation by making him laugh. If we are successful, as was mentioned, his laughter will induce pleasant feelings in him and thus help him to rise above his feelings of distress. In embarrassment laughter serves the same function, only it is not someone else, but ourself, that gets us to laugh. We "break into the loop" by performing the behavior that is a natural expression of pleasant feelings, in order to induce in ourselves pleasant feelings. Like the person who whistles in the dark to make himself feel more relaxed, we use a behavior to alter our feelings.

In embarrassment, too, there is a social function served by laughter. Because it is a natural expression of amusement, we can use laughter to appear to others as though we are not upset but actually amused by the situation we are in. This use of laughter to feign amusement is perhaps more familiar in polite laughter, where we force a laugh, say at our boss's joke, so that he will think that we enjoy his sense of humor. Since laughter is contagious, moreover, by laughing in an embarrassing situation we tend to make others laugh. This has the effect of making them relax, and perhaps even enjoy the situation; where we have been "caught in the act" it tends to defuse their anger and blame, and even where we just want to ask a favor, it "softens them up" for our request.

We are not saying here that an embarrassed person will always, or even usually, think about all the effects that his laughter will have, and consciously force a laugh in order to achieve them. Like other pieces of behavior that have an effect on our state of mind and on other people's attitudes toward us, laughter in embarrassing situations is learned very early in life, and then not by any rational calculation but simply by experience with what kinds of behavior improve uncomfortable situations. By the time we reach adulthood, most of us laugh in embarrassing situations quite automatically. Indeed, some very insecure people who exhibit a great deal of nervous laughter in social situations are hardly conscious that they are doing so.

If laughter is seldom consciously chosen as a coping technique in embarrassing situations, it is not chosen at all in hysteria, where it functions as an involuntary mechanism for reacting to a catastrophe that is too overwhelming for the person to handle, cognitively and emotionally, in any normal way. The shock is even too great to handle by ordinary crying, which, though it is an expression of distress, still involves some rational control of one's behavior, and so is still "normal" in some sense. In hysterical laughter, which often alternates with hysterical crying, the person is not merely very disturbed by what has happened, but is completely overcome by it, so that all rational control is lost. That is why, of course, we consider the person at least temporarily insane.

By reacting with laughter the hysterical person is rejecting the reality of the shocking situation. He is unable to face the horror, and so his nervous system takes over with a behavior that expresses not horror but amusement. If the person speaks, it may well be to deny that the situation is horrible—"No, she's not dead, she's not dead, she can't be dead!" The laughter reinforces this make-believe; if my behavior is expressive of amusement, the unconscious logic seems to be, the situation I am in cannot be a horrible one. In a sense this laughter and rejection of reality "works," for it gives the person some distance, at least temporarily, from the horror; just as hysterical paralysis may "work" for a person who cannot face a certain situation in which he has to use his limbs, by eliminating the need for him to face that situation. The marvelous thing is how these mechanisms operate below the level of conscious thinking. Humor, as we shall see in Chapter 8, can have a similar effect of "distancing," though at a much more conscious level where we gain control over ourselves and our situation.

Hysterical laughter, then, although not voluntary, is nonetheless a *human, psychological* response. But some involuntary laughter is not a psychological response. Laughter is sometimes caused by disorders in the brain such as hypothalamic lesions in multiple sclerosis or epilepsy, or by the use of certain drugs. There are even diseases like the fatal *kuru* in New Guinea, whose primary effect is uncontrollable laughter. While it was necessary for our theory to say something about hysterical laughter, however, we do not have to account for these cases of physiologically induced laughter, any more than an account of crying would have to explain crying while peeling onions. Laughter, as we have set out to account for it, is a human behavior that is a reaction of the person to his perceptions of the world around him—a motor response, to put it crudely, to sensory input. Where the movements of laughter are caused directly by the action of certain drugs or abnormal electrical impulses in the brain, we have an interesting physiological phenomenon but not laughter as a piece of human behavior.

We do have to account for cases like laughter under the influence of nitrous oxide, however, where though chemical changes affect brain physiology, they cause laughter not directly but by bringing about a psychological shift. Most often drugs such as nitrous oxide, marijuana, and alcohol lead to laughter by changing the way the person feels about himself and what is going on around him. On rare occasions they may produce double vision or hallucinations, an actual perceptual shift; but usually they alter the "way we see things" in a different sense. The person may suddenly feel dissociated from the practical aspects of the situation he is in: what had been important or urgent no longer is; if he felt tense or anxious, he no longer does. The sudden onset of this carefree feeling can itself be pleasant enough to trigger laughter. In any case, once in this altered mood, things look different to the person. Objects that normally go unnoticed may become fascinating; the simplest experiences may surprise and delight him. Small incongruities, which would not strike him as funny in his ordinary moods, can be very amusing. Laughter under mood-altering drugs, then, can be nonhumorous laughter, but is often humorous laughter, even though an objective observer might not see what is funny to the person. We might describe both non-humorous and humorous laughter in altered moods by saying that, by objective standards of the stimulation required to trigger laughter, the person has a much lower threshold of amusement. This giddiness can be brought on, we should note, not only by drugs but also by natural chemical processes occurring in the brain, as when a person is overtired.

Our formula that laughter is an expression of pleasure at a psychological shift, then, can be seen to cover even the problem cases on our list. Because laughing is not only a natural expression of pleasure, but is also under our voluntary control, and even under the control of unconscious coping mechanisms, it can occur in the absence of pleasure. I can force a laugh to please my boss or to make myself feel less tense. But such cases, as we saw, are parasitic on laughter as the natural expression of pleasure, for they all work by using laughter to feign pleasure, or by breaking into the causal loop between pleasure and laughter to induce pleasure by performing laughter. Because laughter is partially voluntary, too, it can not only be forced when the person is not amused, but can also be suppressed when he is amused. (Probably the most curious case of laughter suppression is in persons afflicted with cataplexy, a disease in which the patient will lose control of his voluntary muscles and collapse on the floor if he allows himself to laugh.) There is no one-to-one correspondence, in short, between instances of amusement and in-stances of laughter. Nonetheless, our formula that laughter is the natural expression of amusement provides the key to understanding all cases of laughter.

# 6

# The Variety of Humor

Our first five chapters were devoted to a general account of laughter in the many situations in which it is found. From here on we will narrow our focus to those laughter situations which are called humor. In this chapter we will explore some of the many kinds of humor, and in later chapters the importance of humor in human life.

What distinguishes humor from simpler kinds of laughter stimuli, as we have seen, is that it is based on a conceptual shift, a jolt to our picture of the way things are supposed to be. And, as we saw in tracing the development of humor in children, this shift may be based on simple surprise or on incongruity. In humor of simple surprise, the person is confronted with some thing or event of a new kind, which he cannot assimilate into any familiar conceptual category. This kind of humor is common in children, but not in adults. Adults have not only wider experience but a capacity for more abstract concepts, so that almost anything they might experience will count as being of a kind of thing or event they have experienced before.

Most adult humor, then, is based on incongruity and not on simple surprise. Perhaps the most important thing to note about incongruity is that a thing or event is not incongruous *simpliciter*, but only relative to someone's conceptual scheme. Incongruity is a violation of a pattern in someone's picture of how things should be. What any individual finds incongruous will depend on what his experience has been and what his expectations are. If an intelligent being from another galaxy visited Earth and were confronted with a situation which we consider funny (incongruous), he would not find it incongruous unless he had had experience with similar situations before and so had some expectations for what situations of this type are supposed to be like. Without such expectations, at most, the visitor would find our comic situation "funny" only in the more basic way that he finds Earth situations in general funny—they are new to him and so evoke simple surprise.

We do not need to imagine visitors from other planets to understand how an appreciation of humor of incongruity depends on an appropriate conceptual background. (Since the humor of incongruity is the only kind I will be talking about from now on, I will use the term "humor" to mean the humor of incongruity.) Our own children often fail to get certain kinds of adult humor because they lack the requisite conceptual patterns. This applies not just to sophisticated verbal play and to sexual humor, but even to many instances of humor based on adult social conventions, sarcasm, etc. The disparity between the child's naive picture of the world and the adult's sophisticated picture also explains why adults often find children's speech and behavior so amusing, even when the children are not trying to be funny.

Adults from different cultures often fail to appreciate each other's humor, because they don't have the same picture of the world and so do not find the same things incongruous. This is why a joke is often not funny when it is translated into another language. What Wittgenstein said about language-games—that to share a language-game is to share a form of life—applies nicely to humor. To share humor with someone we need to share a form of life with him.

Not only do we not appreciate the humor of very different cultures, but we often find humorous their *ordinary* customs. Many raised in traditional Western culture have found the customs of so-called primitive peoples amusing, but we should remember that it works the other way as well. This ethnocentrism of what we find incongruous is captured nicely in a story told by Margaret Mead. A Plains Indian had just placed food on a new grave, when a white man looking on jocularly asked, "Do you expect the dead man to come up and eat that food?" To which the Indian responded, "As soon as your dead come up to smell the flowers you place on their graves."[1]

What different people find funny also varies between different stages in the history of a single culture. It may be hard for us to imagine today, but when the use of the fork was introduced into England a few hundred years ago, people found this new eating instrument extremely funny. Even the technique of vaccination against smallpox was greeted with a great deal of ridicule. In looking back at the dress and customs of previous generations, too, of course, we are often amused because they differ from our own.

And not only do the individual things and situations which a culture finds funny vary over time, but the whole style of humor may change. Consider, for example, the difference between contemporary cartoons and the cartoon in Figure 2 on the opposite page from *Harper's New Monthly Magazine,* January 1880.

There are variations, also, in what individual adults in a single culture at any given time find humorous; one's educational level, social class, profession, sex, etc., can all make a difference here. As any after-dinner speaker knows, the jokes that would go over big at a meeting of academics might not go over at all at a meeting of a labor union. And there is a noticeable difference between the cartoons in, say, the *New Yorker* and the *National Enquirer.* There are even differences in what individuals find funny based on their unique personalities and perspectives. To explore all the different factors that influence the individual's sense of humor, however, would require much more space, and much more empirical data, than we have available. The few details we have given here will have to suffice as illustrating our main point—that what a person finds incongruous depends on what he finds congruous, and that the latter is based on the conceptual patterns which have been built up in his experience.

We can turn now to investigate some of the different ways in which laughter stimuli may involve incongruity. Perhaps the most basic distinction to be made here is between incongruity in some object or situation, and incongruity in the way a person represents a situation. For convenience we can call these two "incongruity in things" and "incongruity in presentation." One way to see this dis-

MR. VAN PURCELESS BEING FASHIONABLY SHORT OF FUNDS, HAS TO WRITE A CAREFULLY WORDED LETTER, WITH A VIEW TO RAISING THE WIND, AND IS ASSISTED IN THE FOLLOWING MANNER BY HIS SON AND HEIR:

"Pa, will you buy me a plate of ice-cream next Fourth of July?"

"Pa, what does inc-ompr-ehens-ib-le spell?"

"Pa, is it wicked to say 'Confound you'?"
"Confound you—yes! Don't bother!"

"Pa, my nose itches."
"Then scra-a-atch it!"

"Pa, I think the ice-man is going to call for his bill to-day."

This is more than flesh and blood can stand. Van Purceless is on the war-path.

tinction is to contrast two kinds of comic entertainment. A comedian, it has been said, is someone who says funny things—essentially
a teller of jokes—while a comic is someone who says things funny.
Red Skelton is a good example of the former, George Carlin of the
latter. Sometimes this distinction is expressed as the distinction between "humor" and "wit": humor, one writer says, "consists primarily
in what is observed, whereas wit originates in the observer."[2] Because
I am using the term "humor" to cover both these phenomena, however, I will not put the distinction in this way.

Using the general categories of "incongruity in things" and "incongruity in presentation," we can explore some different kinds of
humor. Let's begin with incongruity in things.

Virtually any violation of what a person sees as the standard
order of things can be funny to someone. It has been claimed, by
Bergson and Freud among others, that only what is human or what is
personified by our imagination can be seen as humorous, but this is
not the case. If, as I mentioned earlier, I find a bowling ball in my
refrigerator, I may find this incongruous situation funny, even though
I do not see the ball as a person. Similarly, I can pass by a row of
houses, all of one design, and then laugh on reaching a house of a
completely different design. Any incongruity, whether in human
beings or not, can be seen as funny.

Perhaps the simplest kind of incongruity in things, and the one
that most often makes us laugh, is some deficiency in an object or
person, which renders it or him inferior as the kind of thing it is
supposed to be. A scrawny dog, for example, or a dilapidated car,
can be funny in this way. The humorous deficiencies of persons are
more numerous than the deficiencies of things, and can be divided
roughly into four categories: physical deformity, ignorance or stupidity, moral shortcomings, and actions that fail. A word can be said
about each of these, particularly the last.

Physical deformity, underdevelopment, or weakness, is probably
the oldest human deficiency to be found humorous. As far back as
the *Iliad* (Book II) we find humorous descriptions of deformity. There
Thersites is spoken of as "the ugliest man that had come to Ilium. He
had a game foot and was bandy-legged. His round shoulders almost
met across his chest; and above them rose an egg-shaped head,
which sprouted a few short hairs." A good deal of the Greek gods'

laughter was at deformity—the crippled Hephaistos was the laughing-stock of Olympus. Today our moral sensitivity may prevent us from laughing at deformity in real life, but we still laugh at it in the theater, films, cartoons, and jokes. The fat person, the person with the huge nose, the very ugly person, are all stock laugh getters. Indeed, if we look at the costumes of clowns, they are based almost exclusively on deformity.

Closely allied to our laughter at physical deformity is our laughter at ignorance and stupidity. We laugh at children's naiveté partly because it is a type of ignorance. We laugh at the yokel and the village idiot. Whole genres of jokes, such as the now-waning Polish joke, are based on stupidity. We also laugh at the absentminded professor, who is intelligent in theoretical matters, but who is forgetful or doesn't have practical intelligence. A stock way of getting a laugh in a play is to have some character speak or act in ignorance of some fact that we in the audience are aware of. And even a poor joke can provide a laugh if someone listening to it fails to get it—we'll laugh not at the joke, but at his lack of understanding.

Moral shortcomings, too, have been a standard object of laughter throughout history. The miser, the liar, the drunkard, the lazy person, the lecher, the gossip, the coward, the hypocrite—these are all stock comedic characters. Plato even went so far as to say that moral shortcomings were the *only* object of laughter. Though this is an exaggeration, a good deal of our laughter is directed at people's vices. Indeed, in conversation we often get a laugh simply by suggesting that a person is stingier than everyone knows he is, or that he lies more, drinks more, etc.

Our fourth category of humorous deficiencies with persons—actions that fail—often overlaps with the other three categories, for deformity, stupidity, and vice are often manifested in what people do. But there are humorous possibilities, too, in actions that fail not because of any shortcoming in the person, but because of a defect in someone or something else (e.g., a defective tool), or because of a chance event (e.g., a sudden thunderstorm). Whenever someone is trying to achieve some goal, that is, it can be funny if he fails.

Even when an action does not fail, it can be incongruous, and so humorous, when it is not carried out relatively smoothly. The awkward action, the interrupted action, the action performed by someone who is disorganized or distracted, are all stock devices in comedy. Superfluous gestures in an action can also be funny, because they do not contribute to the goal at hand. A classic example would be the lavish arm movements of the character Ed Norton (Art Carney), on the television series "The Honeymooners," whenever he was about to write a letter, make a pool shot, etc. The humor in these pointless gestures was always heightened by the angry reaction they got from Norton's impatient friend Ralph (Jackie Gleason).

The humor in practical jokes, too, is in large part based on incongruity in actions, only here someone is deliberately causing the failure of the action. In the typical practical joke someone engineers the situation so that another person who is trying to achieve a certain goal will fail or meet with some misfortune. The classic practical joke of removing a person's chair as he attempts to sit down is a paradigm case. "Candid Camera," a popular television show of the 1960s, consisted almost exclusively of practical jokes. In one of their best, a conventional car was fitted with an extra large fuel tank in the trunk and under the rear seat. A woman from "Candid Camera" drove the car into gas stations and asked the attendant to "fill it up." As the gauge on the pump passed the 25-gallon mark, and then the 30- and 40-gallon marks, the attendant would begin to look very concerned—perhaps this car *couldn't* be filled up! A similar stunt involved the driver coasting into a gas station with the engine removed from her car, and asking the attendant to see what was wrong under the hood.

There is another kind of incongruity in actions, which is the reverse of failure. We sometimes laugh when someone *succeeds* in doing something by exerting only a small amount of effort, much less than we would judge necessary to achieve the goal at hand. The plucky hero of the silent film, for example, often got laughs by escaping a very dangerous situation with some simple maneuver that would never work in real life. It is the incongruity of disproportion between effort and result, too, I think, that at least partially explains our laughing when a character like W. C. Fields gets out of a tight spot with a clever lie.

Related to this laughter at serendipity and cleverness is our laughter at situations in which an action fails, but it does not matter to the people involved because they do not even notice. A good example is the joke about the two Englishmen riding on a noisy train. The first says, "I say, is this Wembley?" The other responds, "No, Thursday." To which the first says, "I am too." These two have completely misunderstood each other, but no matter—they *thought* they were communicating.

Deficiencies of various sorts, then, constitute one major kind of incongruity in things. A second kind of incongruity is one thing seeming to be another. When we experience one thing or action A that bears a strong resemblance to another thing or action B, we tend to see A as B. In some instances, as where we have been fooled by a rubber snake and then laugh on discovering that it is only rubber, we may actually have misidentified A as B, and then suddenly seen our mistake. But even where we are not deceived by the B-ness of A into a mistaken judgment that A is B, there is a shift between seeing A as what it is, and seeing it as illuminated by the image of B.

A common form of the incongruity of one thing seeming to be another is the humor of mimicry. The professional comedian doing very realistic impressions of celebrities is only a sophisticated version of what countless peoples all over the world have done for centuries—talking and acting with the intonation, facial expression, and gestures of another person in order to get a laugh.

We also enjoy seeing or hearing about the successful impostor, as long as we are aware, of course, that he is an impostor. The character of the flim-flam man, portrayed so well in the movies by W. C. Fields, is a rich source of comic possibilities. We laugh, too, at the occasional newspaper story about the person who has successfully impersonated a physician, especially if the impostor actually performed a bit of surgery.

The person who pretends to be something other than he is need not be doing so for anyone's amusement; he need not even be consciously aware of his own pretense. We often find people funny who "put on airs," who act as if they are richer or more important than they really are, and in doing so take themselves completely seriously. Indeed, their inflated opinion of themselves makes their pretense all the more humorous, because the incongruity is not just between what they are and what they seem to be, but also between what they are and what they think of themselves as being.

67

A thing that seems to be something else can also be funny when there is no pretense involved. We find it humorous to see a person, in a restaurant, say, who looks just like someone we know—if that person turns out to have mannerisms or a voice similar to our friend's, we find that extra humorous. Many comedies depend heavily on unintentional mistaken identity. Even inanimate objects that look like something else can be funny, especially if they look like people or animals. I once took a tour of a brewery, which ended up on an observation deck above the bottling room. When I looked down at the thousands of bottles on the conveyor lines jockeying for position to get filled, to go through the capping machine, and then to get plunked into cartons, I broke into laughter. All these bottles, which I normally see as inert glass containers, suddenly seemed *alive*, like little soldiers going through some sort of very fast induction process. If we are not overcome by feelings of frustration, we can even enjoy situations in which machines seem to be actively frustrating our efforts to use them; we might even be amused by the string of traffic lights which seem for all the world to be conspiring to keep us from reaching our destination on time.

A third kind of incongruity in things is coincidence. If we happened to run into a friend who told us that he just had his appendix out, for example, this by itself would not be humorous. But if the next two people we talked to told us that they just had the same operation, we might well find this funny. Appendicitis, we assume, is a random occurrence, and the odds against any three particular individuals experiencing it at the same time are very great. And so it is incongruous that we should run into three recent appendectomy patients in a row. Comedies often use the unexpected repetition of events and even lines to get a humorous effect, as when in Molière's *Le Tartuffe* the maid Dorine confronts first one and then the other of a pair of lovers, and each expresses a grievance against the other in virtually the same words (act 2, scene 4). Unimaginative people often try to get a laugh in a similar way, by repeating some current catch phrase all day long in each successive situation. Our amusement at unexpected repetition, too, I think, provides an answer to Pascal's question: Why do we find identical twins funny? We expect people, especially adults, to be unique, and so when we find two that look alike—especially if they are dressed alike—we are surprised. As Bergson says, identical twins look as if they were manufactured; and human beings are the last thing we expect to look this way.

In the humor of coincidence or unexpected repetition, then, there need be nothing funny about the individual things or events; what is incongruous, and therefore funny, is their juxtaposition. The same is true with a fourth kind of incongruity—the juxtaposition of opposites. By itself, a St. Bernard dog is not funny. Nor is a Mexican chihuahua. But when two such dogs are seen together, as in the hackneyed *National Enquirer* photos, they are funny. Similarly, there need be nothing funny about people from the upper class or people from the lower class, but countless comedies have made use of the humorous possibilities in juxtaposing them. A long line of comedy teams, including Laurel and Hardy and Burns and Allen, have exaggerated their physical and psychological differences precisely to get this effect of incongruity.

To get an incongruous juxtaposition, we need not join opposites; in the case of the bowling ball in the refrigerator, for example, what was funny was simply that two things were put together that had no connection with each other. The bowling ball, which fits perfectly well into certain settings, had been placed into a setting where it didn't belong at all. We could count the presence of things in inappropriate situations as a fifth kind of humorous incongruity, but this category would surely be very wide and would partially overlap our other categories. Perhaps it is best to stop our cataloguing here and treat the kinds of incongruity we have cited so far not as an exhaustive list, but simply as illustrations from a potentially infinite list. To be sure, there are kinds of incongruity we have not discussed—the violation of physical laws in cartoons comes to mind here. But once we understand that wherever there is a regularity or pattern in a person's picture of things, there is room for incongruity when that pattern is violated, we can continue the list for ourselves.

Earlier in this chapter we distinguished between incongruity in things and incongruity in presentation. Having explored several examples of the first, we can turn to the second. Incongruity in presentation, as mentioned earlier, is not so much found as created; it lies not so much in the matter at hand as in the way a person presents the matter.

There are several levels at which incongruity can be found in any medium of communication. However, since spoken and written language is by far the most common medium, we will limit our discussion pretty much to them. The lowest level of incongruity in language involves merely the sounds of the spoken word or the shape of the written word, apart from the word's meaning. Excessive alliteration, for example, is incongruous and so potentially humorous, as are multiple rhymes and the weak internal rhymes used by humorists like Ogden Nash. Deliberate or accidental mistakes in pronunciation, spelling, grammar, or other nonsemantic aspects of language, can also be funny. Verbal slips and spoonerisms, for instance, are humorous even when they don't result in new, unintended words. And dialect jokes usually rely for a good deal of their effect on being told with mispronounced words and broken grammar.

We also enjoy playing with syllables, as in speaking Pig Latin, "Op-talk," and other play languages. We can abuse morphemic patterns to get sentences like "If it's feasible, let's fease it," and P. G. Wodehouse's "He may not have been actually disgruntled, but he was certainly far from gruntled."

Like other linguistic patterns, rules of syntax can be violated; but because such violations tend to destroy sense, there are not many pieces of humor based on violations of syntax. (We can play with syntax without violating it, as in jokes whose syntax makes them ambiguous, or as in the following joke, which was popular in Eastern Europe in the 1960s: "Under capitalism, man exploits man. Under communism it is vice versa.")

At the next higher level we have humor which involves the meanings of the words to some extent, but which still depends heavily on the phonological and typographical mechanics of language. Jokes that turn on the use of homonyms fall into this category, as do pronunciation and spelling errors that result in unintended words. But perhaps the most common form of this kind of humor is the simple pun in which a person uses a certain word in a conversation because it has a secondary meaning that is also somehow connected to the topic at hand (or has a homonym so connected). If we are talking about football, for example, someone might say, usually with emphasis on the punning word, "Let's *pass* on to talk about something else." Because such puns involve little cleverness or insight, and because the punster often has to strain the conversation to make his pun, many people have a strong dislike for puns; hence their reputation as "the lowest form of humor." Especially tiresome can be the punning contest, in which everyone gets in on the act by racking his brains for words related to the topic, or homonyms of such words, and then building essentially meaningless comments around them. And for every person who detests puns and tries to quash such games, it seems that there are many more lovers of puns to keep the game going. Some people, indeed, have a mania for punning. King James I was so fond of puns that he required them of his courtiers.

Puns need not be as simple as the example just cited. Though I am a staunch opponent of puns in general, I can appreciate the occasional one that shows cleverness, especially if it is used to actually say something, and not just to keep the punning game going. Perhaps my favorite was a short dramatic review of the play *I Am a Camera,* which read simply: "No Leica."

Somewhat cleverer than the simple pun is the double entendre. As in the simple pun, a word or phrase is used that has two meanings. But here both of the meanings fit into the sentence to make grammatical sense. The sense of "pass" in which we pass a football cannot be given to the word in "Let's pass on to talk about something else." But in a double entendre there is true semantic ambiguity to the sentence as a whole. Consider the story about the English bishop who received the following communication from one of the vicars in his diocese: "My Lord, I regret to inform you of my wife's death. Can you possibly send me a substitute for the weekend."[3] Not only are there two meanings for "substitute," but each gives us a different way of interpreting the sentence.

As this example shows, the humorous double entendre plays on meanings that are not just *different,* but in some way *opposed* to each other. Often the opposition is between a nonsexual meaning and a sexual meaning, particularly when the sexual meaning is taboo. Ambiguous sentences that have different, but not opposed, meanings are not likely to be humorous. When we hear a sentence like "I saw the bank from the bridge," for example, we may be sensitive to the fact that, out of context, "bank" here could refer to a river bank or to a financial institution, but this ambiguity is not likely to amuse us.

Similar in effect to the double entendre are the mispronunciation, the spoonerism, the verbal slip, and the typographical error that result in a second meaning for the sentence. Here again it is opposed, and not simply different, meanings that we find most humorous; though of course we may simply laugh because a mistake has been made. Perhaps we find such errors funniest when we think of them as "Freudian slips," as revelations of what the person would really like to say, but feels constrained not to.

Like the verbal errors above, mistranslations can be humorous simply as errors, but are more humorous when they yield a new meaning that is somehow opposed to the original. For example, the Biblical phrase "The spirit is willing but the flesh is weak" was once translated into the Russian equivalent of "The liquor is good but the food is bad." A good deal of the humor here comes from the contrast between the religious profundity of the original and the secular triviality of the translation.

The kinds of humor in language we have been considering thus far have been based on incongruities in the simpler aspects of language, such as pronunciation, spelling, and the assignment of meaning to words. But, as we move up to higher forms of what we have called humor of presentation, we find incongruities not so much in the "mechanics" of language as in what is being said, the message that the language is being used to convey. While puns and lower forms of humor are basically playing with words, the higher forms of humor, or "wit" as it has traditionally been called, is basically playing with ideas. William Hazlitt described wit as "an arbitrary juxtaposition of dissonant ideas, for some lively purpose of assimilation or contrast, generally of both."[4] The witty comment will often consist of an amusing comparison of two things that normally would not be thought of as similar. When Aristophanes describes a certain statesman as having a voice like a pig on fire, for example, we experience a kind of pleasurable surprise at thinking of the man in these unfamiliar terms.

The resemblance appealed to in the witty comment cannot be too close, or it will tend to be obvious and so not surprising. Nor can it be too distant. After all, everything is similar to everything else in some respect or other. If we pick out only a nonessential or a very general feature that two things have in common, this is not likely to have much effect on our listener. A witty comparison will pick out a feature that is somehow essential in or characteristic of the things being compared, will, as Locke says, find striking and unexpected resemblances.[5]

Though wit is often based on similarities between things, it can take other forms as well. Sometimes the witty comment achieves its effect by looking at a situation from an incongruous point of view. To understand the comment we have to shift to that point of view from our ordinary one; doing so amuses us and we express our amusement in laughter. A character in a comedy of Labiche, for instance, shouts up to his neighbor, who has dirtied his balcony, "What do you mean by emptying your pipe on my terrace?" The man responds, "What do you mean by putting your terrace under my pipe?" The new perspective the pipe smoker has playfully adopted here is absurd, of course, but as long as we can understand what that perspective is, we can be amused by his comment. More often the shift in perspective in humor is not to an absurd point of view, but only to one which we do not ordinarily adopt, as in Oscar Wilde's turnaround of an old saying: "Work is the curse of the drinking classes." Comics have created many very funny routines simply by taking ordinary situations and asking us to view them from the perspective of, say, an animal or a visitor from space.

Another humorous device related to the shift in perspective is play with categories, describing something in one category as if it were in another. There is a scene in Woody Allen's *Annie Hall* in which Allen goes into a room to kill a spider and comes out with a very troubled look on his face. "You've got a spider in there the size of a Buick," he says, "definitely a *major* spider." What's funny here is not just the comparison of the spider to something very large—a car—but Allen's use of a specific brand name of car. "A spider the size of a car" would not have been nearly as funny as the line used, because it would have involved merely exaggeration. But by using the expression "the size of a Buick," Allen has shifted categories from talk of physical objects of different sizes to talk of cars. For something to be "the size of a Buick" it has to be a motor vehicle or something of the sort. But, of course, spiders are not in this category at all. A similar category shift makes Allen's use of the phrase "*major* spider" funny, too. In taxonomy, spiders categorized as major would be larger than other spiders; but Allen's pronunciation of the word "major" indicates that he means more than that. Allen's meaning is that this spider is of great *importance*, as, say, a major fire or a major earthquake would be. And ordinary spiders simply aren't in this category.

Though most instances of devices like the shift in perspective and the category shift are verbal, we should point out that they may be visual. Charles Addams's cartoon (Figure 3) works by treating figures from paintings as if they were real people. Many devices in verbal humor can be translated into a visual medium. The sight gags in Woody Allen's movies, for instance, often look as if they started out as jokes.

Returning now to verbal humor and the kinds of incongruity it employs, we find another rich source of incongruity in the violation of logical principles. What seems to work best here is not a complete lack of logic in a piece of reasoning, but rather a violation of some logical principle in a piece of reasoning that is just logical enough to sound somewhat plausible. In Mark Twain's *Innocents Abroad*, the author offers his homage at the Tomb of Adam: "The tomb of Adam! How touching it was here in a land of strangers, far from home . . . to discover the grave of a blood relation. . . I leaned upon a pillar and burst into tears. . . Noble old man—he did not live to see me." The incongruity here is in the illogic of Twain's reasoning; far from being "a blood relation," Adam is his *most distant* relative. But what makes Twain's tribute especially funny is the ring of plausibility it has. Indeed, in some pieces of humor based on logical incongruities, it may take some logical expertise to figure out just where the reasoning goes wrong. Almost everyone would agree that the following graffiti is invalid as a syllogism, but few are able to put their finger on the mistake involved.

> A stale pretzel is better than nothing.
> Nothing is better than God.
> Therefore, a stale pretzel is better than God.

Some pieces of humor even work a logical incongruity into an interchange between two characters so that not only is the incongruity accepted as if it made sense, but the person responding to the incongruous line actually builds on the incongruity. In the Marx Brothers' *Animal Crackers*, for instance, Chico says to Groucho, "He thinks I

"I think you know everybody."

look alike," to which Groucho responds, "Well, if you do, it's a tough break for both of you."

An interesting genre of humor based on the violation of logical principles is the Irish bull. Sometimes these are close to things people actually say, and what is at fault is not the person's reasoning so much as the way he expresses himself, as in the following:

> Policeman: "Say you! If you're going to smoke here, you'll have to either put out your pipe, or go somewhere else."

The logical mistake here is certainly no worse than that made by an Omaha woman who, when asked by an interviewer about her television-watching habits, said, "Oh, I never watch TV. I turn it off more than I turn it on."

Yet often in Irish bulls it is not just the wording but the reasoning that is incorrect, as in:

> Irishman: "Be gorra I wisht I knew the place where I am goin' to die, and sure and I'd niver go there!"

Another kind of humor is based, not on the violation of logic, but on a spurious appeal to logical or quasilogical principles. In one of Myron Cohen's best jokes, a man is in bed in the afternoon with his neighbor's wife, when suddenly they hear her husband coming through the front door. The man jumps out of bed and scrambles into the closet, where he buries himself under some clothes, shoes, and other closet odds and ends. The suspicious husband bursts in through the bedroom door and shouts, "Okay, where is he?" He looks under the bed, behind the draperies, in the bathroom, and then finally in the closet. When he at last pulls away the paraphernalia covering the man, he triumphantly asks, "And what are *you* doing here?" To which the man replies, "Everybody's got to be *some*place."

Statements can be humorous, too, when they sound informative, but are actually just tautologies. Here are two examples:

> Everything tastes more or less like chicken.
> You can get anywhere in 10 minutes if you go fast enough.

Conversely, a statement can be amusing when it sounds tautologous, and perhaps even is, but is somehow illuminating nonetheless. The maxim "A rich man is just a poor man with money" is like that, as are many pieces of folk wisdom.

Paradoxes are often amusing in a similar way: at first they appear to be necessarily false, because self-contradictory; but then we see that the contradiction is only apparent and that the statement actually reveals something true. According to a story told about Picasso, an art dealer bought a canvas signed "Picasso" and travelled to Cannes to see if it was genuine. Picasso took one look and said, "It's a fake." A few months later the man bought another canvas signed "Picasso" and returned to Cannes. Again Picasso said, "It's a fake." "But *cher maitre*," the man protested, "it so happens that I saw you with my own eyes working on this very painting several years ago." Picasso simply shrugged his shoulders and replied, "I often paint fakes."

The last kind of linguistic humor we will consider is based on the breaking of pragmatic rules, the rules governing the use of language in particular communication situations. Pragmatic incongruity may come into our use of language, first of all, in the connection between an assertion and the state of affairs it purports to refer to. When someone makes a statement that we know is a gross exaggeration or an outright lie, we may be amused by the "lack of fit" between the statement and reality. Tall tales in fiction can be funny in a similar way. When we hear about the amazing feats of someone like Paul Bunyan, we may laugh because we know that no human could perform such feats. Exaggeration of what is possible sometimes combines with logical incongruity, as in Carl Sandburg's yarn about the man who was so tall that he had to climb a ladder to shave himself.

A related kind of incongruity exists between the semantic content of someone's utterance and the tone, gestures, or facial expression with which he speaks it. We find it funny to listen to someone read a serious speech, for example, with an insufficiently serious tone, or with an overly grave one, or with inappropriate gestures or facial expressions. Sarcasm is often funny because it is clear from the way the person is saying what he says that he doesn't mean it. Sometimes too, as in humorous understatement and overstatement, it can be obvious simply from the situation that the person is being ironic. On a Monday morning a condemned man was being led to the scaffold, the story goes, when he said, "What a lousy way to start the week!"

Written language can be funny when there is an incongruity between the message and the way it is expressed. Gag signs such as "THIMK" and "ESCHEW OBFUSCATION" work by violating the very maxim they express. And signs such as "Want to learn to read? Call 458-1000" are funny because they could not serve as a message to their intended audience. A real life example of this second kind of incongruity is the sign on the doors of post offices, "No dogs allowed, except seeing-eye dogs."

Another area of pragmatics that is a rich source of humor is presupposition. Linguists and philosophers have discussed presupposition a great deal in recent years, and have used the word in different ways. For our purposes, we can say that when utterance U presupposes proposition P, then P has to be true in order for U to be used successfully. The command "Close the door," for instance, presupposes such propositions as "There is a door to which I am referring" and "The door is open." Unless there is a door and it is open, "Close the door" cannot be used as a command—if these words are uttered, as Austin says, they will "misfire."

One way to get incongruity from an utterance that has presuppositions is simply to use it when we know that it will "misfire," that is, when it is obvious that the presupposed propositions are false. For instance, on arriving home after a busy day a woman might say to her husband, "I'm exhausted—let's call the White House and tell them we can't make it." A sophisticated joke of this type is Martin Mull's "Do you realize that man is the only animal that chews the ice in its drink?" For this to serve as a real piece of information, there would have to be several species that had iced drinks. There aren't, of course, and so this is just a piece of silliness.

Another way to play with presupposition is to use an utterance, usually a question, which presupposes something that is false, but not obviously so, and which is nonetheless embarrassing to the person to whom it is addressed. Asking someone, "Do you still pick your nose all the time?" presupposes that at least in the past the person did frequently pick his nose. By uttering this question we give the impression that it is common kowledge that he had, and still might have, this nasty habit. Lots of hostile and mock hostile humor works in this way by putting the hostile content not in the utterance, but in what the utterance presupposes. Johnny Carson, on the "Tonight Show," once said to Ed McMahon, after McMahon had corrected him on his pronunciation of some word, "Well, I'm sure that Dirward Kirby won't be like that when he's sitting there." If Carson had put the playfully hostile content into what his utterance *said*, if his statement had been "I'm going to replace you with Dirward Kirby," then his utterance wouldn't have been very funny. But by making a statement that *presupposed* that McMahon was being replaced, Carson made it sound as though everyone could just assume that he was firing McMahon, which in the situation was quite funny.

Though there are many more aspects to the pragmatics of language, and thus many more places where humorous incongruity can be worked into our use of language, we cannot hope to examine them all here. I have been trying merely to touch on a few of the major kinds of pragmatic incongruity. There is, however, one other class of incongruity we should consider before bringing this discussion to a close, and that is incongruity based on violation of the general guidelines governing conversation. Like the topic of presupposition, the principles of conversation have come up for a lot of attention in recent years. Perhaps the most fruitful way to proceed is to list some of the principles that have been articulated, and then show how the violation of each has humorous possibilities.

In a well-known paper entitled "Logic and Conversation,"[6] H. P. Grice presents his view that conversation is a rational procedure, basically an exchange of information and opinion, which is guided at the most general level by what he calls "the Cooperative Principle." Because of the cooperative and rational nature of conversation, he says, participants in a conversation can be expected to follow such guidelines as the following:

1. Make your contribution as informative as is required for the current purposes of the exchange.
2. Do not make your contribution more informative than is required.
3. Do not say what you believe to be false.
4. Do not say that for which you lack adequate evidence.
5. Avoid obscurity of expression.
6. Avoid ambiguity.
7. Be brief.
8. Be orderly.

Now clearly, as children learning to talk, we do not memorize these principles and then recite them to ourselves each time we are about to enter a conversation. They are hardly ever learned as explicit formulae; rather they are simply picked up as part of the technique in learning the art of conversation. By the same token, when we violate these principles for some humorous effect, we don't say to ourselves, "Now I'll break the rule against prolixity." As with the other linguistic techniques of humor we have discussed, the violation of conversational principles works mostly at the level of our implicit knowledge of how language, in its serious uses, is supposed to operate.

Let us look at the principles one at a time, to see their humorous possibilities.

*1. It is often funny when a person's contribution to a conversation is not informative enough.* Someone's giving one-word answers to questions that clearly call for more, is a stock comedic device. So is the person's giving an evasive answer in order to keep something hidden. The latter device is often funniest when the person merely repeats the question a number of times—"Me, who, *me*? What am *I* doing with your wallet?"

*2. The person who gives too much information is likewise a stock comic character.* To respond to a simple question like "How have you been?" with five minutes' worth of tedious details on every aspect of one's daily life is clearly not to cooperate with the other person, and, in the right situation, can be very funny. Completely obvious information, if it can be called that, is inappropriate too, in most conversations, and so pointing out what everyone already knows can be humorous. A sophisticated version of giving useless information is denying that some state of affairs obtains when no one would have ever thought that it did. One of Johnny Carson's routines, for example, involved his reading off a list of "little known facts," among them the following: "It is impossible to milk a bird," and "There is no mention of anyone named 'Soupy' in the Old Testament."

*3. We are often amused by lies.* Earlier we mentioned the humor possible in the gross exaggeration and the lie, as based on the incongruity between what is asserted and what we know to be the case. Here we might merely add that part of our amusement at the exaggeration or the lie can come from our realization that the other person is deliberately misusing what is supposed to be a medium for the communication of information. Small children can be especially funny when we know that they are lying.

*4. The wild speculation or the guess inserted into a conversation as a straightforward assertion can be funny much as the exaggeration and the lie are.* To assert something is to give others to believe that one knows what one is talking about. When it is discovered that one has merely been "talking through his hat," again there is the realization that language has been misused, and in the right circumstances this in-

80

congruity can be amusing. The person who pretends expertise in fields he knows little about is often a funny figure.

5. *Obscurity of expression humorously hinders, or in some cases, prevents communication.* For someone to be sending a message in such a form that the person for whom it is intended cannot receive it is incongruous, and so can be humorous. Sometimes, as when we read or listen to bureaucratic gobbledegook, our amusement is heightened by our feeling that the obscure language may well be a smokescreen to hide the writer's or speaker's incompetence.

6. *Ambiguity can be used deliberately.* We discussed earlier some of the humorous possibilities of ambiguity. We might add here that our amusement at someone's use of ambiguous language can be heightened, as in the previous case, by the feeling that the person is deliberately trying *not* to communicate.

7. *Long-windedness in one's contribution to a conversation works against the cooperative nature of conversation.* It tends to turn a dialog into a speech (or, if the others get so fed up that they stop listening, into a monolog). As long as we're not trying to interrupt the windbag or conversation-monopolizer, however, we may find him funny, because his failure to treat the conversation as a cooperative venture makes his behavior incongruous.

8. *All conversation is somewhat disorderly.* One person will start talking before the other has stopped, a speaker will start a sentence and then in midsentence switch to a new one, the topic will sometimes change rather abruptly, etc. Within certain limits this disorder can be tolerated. But when the interruptions are too frequent, when the false starts pile up within a single sentence, and topic changes come too thick and fast, then the conversation gives way to confusion. When this happens, either in one participant's speech or in the conversation as a whole, it is common for people to feel the incongruity of what is happening and break into laughter.

In addition to these eight guidelines, there are other aesthetic, social, and moral principles guiding our talking to one another. There are written and unwritten conventions of politeness, for example. And there are limitations on the topics we may introduce with certain groups of people. Particular speech acts, too, are governed by their own principles. Gordon and Lakoff have suggested that we can make requests reasonably, for instance, only if we have reasons for wanting the request carried out, for assuming that our hearer can do it, would be willing to do it, and would not do it without our request.[7]

The violation of any of these principles has humorous possibilities. The young child who is oblivious of the requirements of politeness and repeats some critical remark made about Aunt Mary to Aunt Mary, the person who starts up a conversation about sex with another for whom the subject is strictly taboo, the person who makes an impossible request just to be silly—all these are found in our everyday humor and have been the stuff of comedy for thousands of years.

In concluding our earlier discussion of incongruity in things, we remarked on the futility of trying to compile an exhaustive list of all kinds of humor based on such incongruity. The same comment applies to incongruity in the violation of conversational guidelines, and more generally, to the whole area of incongruity in presentation. Wherever there is a principle to be violated or regularity to be upset, there is room for incongruity and so for humor. We can even glean humor from the failure of a piece of humor itself. When a joke is told but someone doesn't get it, that situation is often funny. And if a comedian's jokes aren't going over but he reacts in certain ways that emphasize how bad the jokes are, he can often get more laughs than he would have gotten with good jokes. Comedians like Johnny Carson, who have lots of weak material written for them, are adept at getting laughs from this "metahumor."

I would like to conclude this chapter with a brief discussion of three general principles of comic technique that can be distilled from what we have seen so far about the nature of humor. The first is that in order to bring about the shift in humor, the person creating the humor must engage the interest of those he wants to amuse, and thus have some control over their train of thought. One way to do this is to have the funny comment or other stimulus flow from a practical situation in which they are already engaged, as in the wisecrack on the job. In a situation where we are not engaged in some task, as in a night club where we have come to watch a comedian, the humorist must somehow first engage our interest, get us thinking along certain lines, before he can make us laugh. Many comedians establish this initial rapport with the audience by making the same moves we make to start a conversation—they will say "It's nice to be here," will comment on the place they are in, on the weather, etc. Often a comedian will start off his routine by mentioning some ordinary problem that everyone in the audience has faced. When possible, a comedian tells his funny stories as if they really happened, and to him, if that is plausible. (In an anecdote it takes less of an incongruity in the punch line to get a laugh than it does in a joke that we know is made up.) In all these ways, the comedian will get the audience to feel familiar with him and interested in what he's saying, so that he can set them up for the mental shifts of his humor.

A second principle of comic technique is related to the first. Since humor involves a disturbance of our ordinary patterns of thought and expectation, a jolt to our picture of reality, it is important in any extended sequence of humor stimuli, such as a comic monolog or play, to maintain an atmosphere in which the audience's sense of reality is preserved. Creators of humor sometimes fail, paradoxically, because they try to make *everything* funny. But this is impossible, for the incongruity of humor works only by contrast with ordinary patterns of reality. It is self-defeating to set up a "completely wacky, zany, anything-goes" atmosphere, as the movie ads sometimes put it, for when the audience's sense of reality and their ordinary expectations are put in abeyance, it becomes much harder to surprise them with anything that will seem incongruous. A movie where "ANYTHING CAN HAPPEN . . . AND *DOES*!!!" may be amusing for the first few minutes. But as social conventions, standards of reasonable behavior, and even laws of physics are violated over and over with gay abandon, the audience begins to set aside its ordinary expectations, and a situation of diminishing returns takes over. Like the drug addict who is getting acclimatized to the drug he is using, the audience requires progressively higher doses of incongruity for each successive laugh. In the end, tedium usually sets in.

On the other hand, the movie which does not try to be completely wacky, but which stays pretty close to reality and builds its incongruities on plausible events, can be amusing from beginning to end; by preserving our sense of reality and our ordinary expectations, it can jolt us with incongruities again and again. This is the secret behind the comedies of someone like Neil Simon, whose realistic work is usually far funnier than, say, *It's a Mad, Mad, Mad, Mad World.*

The third and last principle of comic technique I want to mention here is the necessity of originality and freshness. If the audience is to experience a mental shift, they must be caught offguard with something that they cannot smoothly assimilate. When we hear an old joke or something we recognize as a variation on an old joke, we are relatively prepared for the punch line, and so it does not have the effect on us intended by the joke teller. Nothing gets stale faster than a joke, and today's witticism is tomorrow's cliché. Like what is fun, what is funny has to surprise us in some way.

The job of the humorist, then, is a challenging one. He or she must have a solid grasp of reality in its manifold patterns, and at the same time be constantly looking at things from new and unusual perspectives. In many ways the humorist's approach is similar to that of a painter, composer, or other artist. Indeed, in our next chapter we'll trace some of these parallels in more detail, and suggest that creating and appreciating humor are at bottom aesthetic activities.

# 7
# Humor as Aesthetic Experience

Having explored some of the many ways in which humor is created or simply found in our experience, I would like to spend the last four chapters considering the role of humor in human life. I am especially concerned to show that humor has a much higher value than it has traditionally been thought to have. In the end, I will suggest, humor is not only distinctively human, but important to human life in a way that nothing else is.

To put our apology for humor in a historical perspective, we need to understand the main lines of criticism that have been offered against it. There are three of these, and they all start with Plato. First, it is charged that in humor we are exposed to something base, viz., human shortcomings, which can "rub off on us." Engaging in humor, therefore, is potentially harmful to one's character. Second, it is said that in laughing at a situation we lose control of our rational faculties and become silly and irresponsible. This loss of our highest faculties, according to Plato, is a loss of what makes us truly human. For this reason he insisted in his *Republic* that "persons of worth" must not be represented in literature or drama as overcome by laughter.[1] And third, following another consequence of Plato's and Aristotle's superiority theories, it is charged that laughter is basically scorn, and so is antisocial and uncharitable.

A negative attitude toward humor and laughter can be found not only in the ancient Greeks, but throughout the classical world and in classical Indian culture.

In the Bible, too, laughter has negative connotations. It is seldom mentioned, but when it is, it is almost always the laugh of derision. The exception is Sarah's laughing when the Lord tells her that she will bear a child in her old age, but here, as the story makes clear, Sarah's laugh is based on her foolishness and failure to believe that God can do all things. Jesus, as many have pointed out, is never represented in the Bible as laughing or enjoying humor.

The Church Fathers said little about the subject, but St. John Chrysostom, the fourth-century Archbishop of Constantinople, gives us a hint of one early Christian view of humor and laughter:

> . . . to laugh, to speak jocosely, does not seem an acknowledged sin, but it leads to acknowledged sin. Thus laughter often gives birth to foul discourse, and foul discourse to actions still more foul. Often from words and laughter proceed railing and insult; and from railing, and insult, blows and wounds; and from blows and wounds, slaughter and murder. If, then, thou wouldst take good counsel for thyself, avoid not merely foul words, and foul deeds, or blows, and wounds, and murders, but unseasonable laughter, itself.[2]

There is little reference to humor and laughter in what survives of medieval literature, but in early modern times we see the same ethical objections already mentioned. Elizabethan playwrights such as Ben Jonson could justify the existence of comedy only on the grounds that Plato gave—that comedy can serve a corrective function by prompting us to avoid the vices portrayed on the stage. Dryden was the first among literary critics of the period to challenge this view and suggest that comedy could be valuable simply in evoking our delight and laughter. But this was not a popular idea. Thomas Shadwell spoke for many when he wrote: "I must take leave to dissent from those who seem to insinuate that the ultimate end of a Poet is to delight without correction or instruction. Methinks a poet should never acknowledge this, for it makes him of as little use to mankind as a fiddler or a dancing master."[3]

When the Puritans succeeded in closing the theaters, it was in large part because of the harmful effects comedies were thought to have on the audience. In a pamphlet published in 1633, William

Prynne put the case against humor and laughter; stage plays produce laughter, he said, usually at some "obscene, lascivious, sinful passage, gesture, speech or jest (the common object of men's hellish mirth) which should rather provoke the Actors, the Spectators to penitent sobs, than wanton smiles; to brinish tears than carnal solace. . ." The person who is laughing is out of control, and laughter is incompatible with the sobriety proper to good Christian men and women, who should not be "immoderately tickled with mere lascivious vanities, or . . . lash out into excessive cachinnations in the public view of dissolute graceless persons."[4]

The late seventeenth and eighteenth centuries saw many condemnations of humor and laughter. Bossuet denounced Molière's comedies and charged that laughter was a tool of the devil. Addison, in the *Spectator* (35), allowed for laughter, but insisted that it should always be under the control of reason. Perhaps the most famous attack on laughter from this period is found in a letter from Lord Chesterfield to his son:

> Having mentioned laughing, I must particularly warn you against it. . . Frequent and loud laughter is the characteristic of folly and ill manners; it is the manner in which the mob express their silly joy at silly things; and they call it being merry. In my mind, there is nothing so illiberal, and so ill-bred, as audible laughter. True wit, or sense, never yet made anybody laugh; they are above it, they please the mind, and give a cheerfulness to the countenance. But it is low buffoonery, or silly accidents, that always excite laughter; and that is what people of sense and breeding should show themselves above. . . I am neither of a melancholy nor a cynical disposition, and am as willing and apt to be pleased as anybody; but I am sure that since I had full use of my reason, nobody has ever heard me laugh.[5]

Baudelaire, in the nineteenth century, spoke of humor as "a damnable element born of satanic parentage."[6] Laughter, he said, was part of the dark side of human nature inherited from Adam's fall; and this is evidenced in part by the fact that "laughter is one of the most frequent symptoms of madness."[7] De Lamennais added an aesthetic argument. Laughter, he said, "never gives to the face an expression of sympathy or good will. On the contrary, it distorts the most harmonious features into a grimace, it effaces beauty, it is one of the images of evil."[8]

In the 1870s two editions of a book entitled *A Philosophy of Laughter and Smiling* were published, in which the author, George Vasey, attempted to show that laughter was not only ethically and aesthetically objectionable, but medically harmful as well. The natural use for the diaphragm and related muscles, he argued, is in breathing. Laughter involves a wholly unnatural and harmful stimulation of these muscles. Circulation of the blood is restricted, breathing is violently interfered with, and sometimes the convulsions of laughter even cause the person's death. Now in our culture, Vasey admitted, almost everyone laughs, but that is because as infants we are stimulated to this unnatural piece of behavior by being poked and tickled. Once we have developed this nasty habit as children, we maintain it into adulthood. "It is very questonable that children would ever begin to laugh if they were not stimulated or prompted, but were let alone, and treated naturally and rationally."[9]

Attacks on humor and laughter have not ceased in our own century. According to Ludovici, whose superiority theory was discussed briefly in Chapter 2, laughter is the act of an inferior person trying to maintain or achieve some status, but without expending much effort to do so. A strong and noble person would never be found laughing.

> Humour is, therefore, the lazier principle to adopt in approaching all questions, and that is why the muddle is increasing everywhere. Because the humorous mind shirks the heavy task of solving thorny problems and prefers to make people laugh about them. . . Truth to tell, there is in every inspired and passionate innovator a haughty energy which is incompatible with the cowardice and indolence of humour.[10]

If all these criticims of laughter and humor seem strangely out of date or like the work of crackpots, we might think back to our own education and try to remember where we might have heard such criticisms before. The traditional attitude of teachers toward laughter and humor, I think it is safe to say, has been that they are frivolous activities that pull us away from what is important. We were in school, as Miss Fidditch so often reminded us, to "do our work," and doing one's schoolwork was part of the larger scheme in which we were to later "do our work," in the factory, office, home, or wherever we found ourselves. Life is fundamentally a serious business—certainly whatever is important in life is serious business. If laughter and humor had any place at all, then, it was not in the classroom but outside somewhere, perhaps as a device for refreshing us to return to our work with more eagerness.

One area where we occasionally could not avoid being exposed to humor in the classroom was in our study of literature, especially drama. But even here, Miss Fidditch (with the backing of traditional literary critics) emphasized that even the best comedies were somehow frivolous and not to be compared in value with tragedies. In our scant exposure to the arts other than literature, there was little problem avoiding the topic of humor, because there was so little humor in the art in the textbooks, and because traditional art criticism says so little about humor. The larger museums show the occasional Magritte, and movements like Funk Art surface from time to time, but for most critics and especially for educators, such work has little artistic significance, and may be viewed simply as art taking a break before returning to the serious business at hand.

I would like to challenge these attitudes I have been describing, for I think that they greatly underestimate the importance of humor in our lives. In the rest of this chapter I want to compare humor with something that *is* highly valued, aesthetic experience. Our enjoyment of a good deal of humor, I shall argue, is a kind of aesthetic experience, and as such is equal in value to any other kind of aesthetic experience.

Perhaps the most basic characteristic shared by humor and aesthetic experience generally is that both have intrinsic value for us. Playing a flute or watching the sun come up are simply enjoyable activities; to do these things we do not need any further justification. Similarly, the delight of sharing a funny comment with a friend or paging through the *New Yorker* for the cartoons is an end in itself.

This self-containedness of aesthetic experience and humor suggests their connection with play, play being in this instance an activity carried out for its own enjoyment. It is this sense, I think, that is behind our talk of "playing" music and "playing" practical jokes on people. If we trace the development of play in children, we notice that the baby starts off life doing almost everything, except crying perhaps, for its own enjoyment—eating because food tastes good, moving its limbs in certain ways because it feels good, exploring the surroundings because it's fun to do. With no responsibilities, the baby spends all its time in activities that are ends rather than means, and in this sense the baby can be said to be playing all the time. As the infant grows through this stage, it will learn which experiences are pleasurable and thus will acquire the foundation for later aesthetic experience, and will begin to laugh when stimulated in certain ways, and thus acquire the foundation for humor.

As the child gets a little older he learns to play in another sense of that word—he learns to mimic and pretend. He plays doggy, and he plays that he is making cookies. In such activities lies a more specialized foundation for drama, dance and the plastic arts, and also for humor. Making believe that he is a dog will be exciting for the child in an aesthetic way. He knows that the characteristics he is adopting do not really belong to him, but there they are in him. Moving around on all fours, barking like a dog, and having co-operative parents treat him like a dog—that kind of playing around with reality is fun. It is also funny. The psychological shift involved in acting like something he is not, and in having people treat him as what he is not, is exhilarating for the child; it delights him, amuses him, makes him laugh.

Later when the child learns more about language and then about pictures, drawing, modeling in clay, and other forms of representation, he will feel the fun of representing all kinds of things, and doing so in any way that pleases him. He can say "Daddy is . . ." and then say "a man," as he has been taught, or he can say "a baby" or even "a doggy." In his coloring book he can make the cat some reasonable cat color like black, or he can choose a color that cats don't come in, like lime green.

This delight in representing things in new ways and taking things as what they are not brings us to another point of comparison between aesthetic experience generally and humor, and that is the importance of imagination in each. In the aesthetic frame of mind we are not locked into looking at things in just one way. We are free to shift our perspective, several times if we choose, see things as other things, and even build fictional worlds. I remember the thrill experienced by a young friend of mine when at the age of two-and-a-half he discovered this power of imagination. I was giving him a ride in the front basket of a bicycle, and I playfully asked, "Could your

90

mommy fit into this basket?" The idea struck him funny, and he laughed with an insistent "Nooo." But then his eyes twinkled and he said, "We could put our *house* in the basket." He chuckled about that for quite awhile, repeating the words several times to reinforce the delicious silliness of the idea. It is this kind of imagination that is at work in much of our aesthetic experience. The artist and the humorist, if they are doing their job well, will surprise us, and often surprise themselves. In art one of the most common ways of praising someone's work is to say that he or she "saw things in a new way." And the same vocabulary is used in praising a humorist—most often used are words like "imaginative," "creative," "inventive," and "original." The child playing doggy or saying that a house can fit into a bicycle basket is at an early stage of both art and humor.

Part of the delight we feel in this use of our imagination is the feeling of liberation it brings. Instead of following well-worn mental paths of attention and thought, we switch to new paths, notice things we didn't notice before, and countenance possibilities, and even absurdities, as easily as actualities. Magritte said that for him art was a visible token of the freedom of human imagination, and except sometimes for the word "visible" we can say the same thing about humor.

I will have more to say about humor and liberation in the next chapter, but the notion of liberation here brings up a related feature of our experience of humor and aesthetic experience generally, the practical disengagement or "distance" in these experiences. It is a familiar idea in aesthetics that to appreciate something aesthetically we must be attending to the object itself and enjoying it for its own sake. If we are looking at a painting we own, for example, and are filled with practical concern for how we might get the best price for it from another collector, then our attention will not be on the painting itself and our experience of it will not be aesthetic experience. Similarly, if in watching a lightning storm from a hilltop, we are suddenly taken with fear by the thought that we are in danger, then our practical concern will override our capacity for simply enjoying the sights and sounds of the storm. Our experience of humor is like this, too. As we saw in Chapter 5, in order to enjoy a psychological shift, and thus to laugh, we need to be without urgent practical needs. If we feel that we are in danger, for example, the most highly incongruous situation will not be apt to amuse us. Finding a cobra in the refrigerator, as we said earlier, is certainly incongruous, and indeed might strike us as funny if we watched someone else do the finding, either in real life or, better (because safer), in a film. But if we are the one opening the door, we probably cannot help but feel practically engaged; and thus we are not able to enjoy the incongruity. Instead we will feel fear, slam the door, and run. Later, when the snake has been removed from the house, we may be able to look back at the incident more as an observer, with the distance of time, and find it funny. Indeed, when old friends reminisce, the events they laugh hardest over were often not funny at all to them while they were occurring.

Not only needs accompanied by negative emotions, but practical motivations generally block amusement. Suppose, for instance, that while walking in the park I see a watch strapped around the branch of a small tree. There are at least two ways I might react. I might simply enjoy the incongruity of this humanoid tree "wearing" a watch. Or I might be motivated by a desire to possess this piece of jewelry—I might see this as an opportunity to pick up a free watch. In the latter case there will be something that has to be done—I have to get the watch off the branch before its owner comes back or anyone else gets it—and my practical engagement in this situation will block my capacity for simply enjoying its incongruity.

Having explored some of the parallels between amusement at humor and aesthetic experience generally, we can turn to the suggestion made earlier that humor is a variety of aesthetic experience. A common way of defining aesthetic experience is as attending to some object of awareness for the sake of the experience itself. An aesthetic object may be something found in nature, or something produced by human beings. If the latter, it may have been produced to be an aesthetic object—what we call "fine art"—or it may have been produced to serve some practical function but happen to be an interesting object in its own right. My speaking of aesthetic *objects* here should not be understood too narrowly. I'm thinking not only of solid physical objects like mountains, paintings, and interestingly shaped machine parts, but also of events like thunderstorms, the performances of dancers, and the movements of certain lawn sprinklers. Works of literature and stories that are passed on orally are also aesthetic objects.

Now our amusement at humor is a kind of aesthetic experience, I suggest, when it is the enjoyment of incongruity for its own sake, the enjoyment of a conceptual shift by itself. Sometimes, as we noted in Chapter 5, humor involves not just a conceptual shift but also an emotional one, as when we enjoy an enemy's clumsy failure at some task because our desires to see him fail and suffer are fulfilled, or when we enjoy some incongruous event because it makes us rich. Now the enjoyment of an emotional shift is neither necessary nor sufficient for humor, as we have seen. Much humor occurs without it, and where an emotional shift is enjoyed by itself, we have not humorous laughter, but the laugh of derision, perhaps, or the laugh of self-glory. (If the only aspect of our enemy's clumsy failure that we enjoy is his failing, then our enjoyment is not a kind of humor.) And where the conceptual shift in humor is accompanied by an emotional shift, then we are not enjoying the incongruous object of our amusement in an aesthetic way, because we are not enjoying it for its own sake alone. Our enjoyment is not focused only on the proper object of amusement—incongruity—but also on such extrinsic considerations as the suffering the incongruous event will bring our enemy, say, or the wealth it will bring us.

Consider a parallel case where a potentially aesthetic experience is rendered nonaesthetic by the admixture of considerations extrinsic to the aesthetic object itself. Imagine a woman gazing at a piece of sculpture she owns with enjoyment. If she is enjoying looking at the shape of the work, its patina, and other intrinsic features, but is also reveling in it because her having such an expensive piece of art makes her friends envious and thus increases her self-esteem, it seems natural to say that her enjoyment of the sculpture is not aesthetic, even though part of her enjoyment arises from her attention to intrinsic properties of the work. Like other kinds of enjoyment, our enjoyment of humor is aesthetic when it is focused on the object itself and when it is disinterested. Our enjoyment of humor is a kind of aesthetic experience, in short, when only the necessary conditions for humor are met, that is, when incongruity is enjoyed for its own sake.

When humor is a kind of aesthetic experience it has an aesthetic object—"object" being understood in the wide sense mentioned earlier—which may be something natural, such as ducks landing on ice, or something produced by humans. If the latter, it may have been produced to be humorous (e.g., a cartoon or a joke), or it may have been produced to serve a practical function but turned out also to be humorous (e.g., Nixon's "Checkers" speech).

Aesthetic experience generally is important in our lives. We need to be able to stop occasionally amid the practical stream of everyday living to simply enjoy attending to things and situations we perceive or imagine. And enjoying humor is one way we do this. But humor does not serve merely as a pause in our practical lives; as we will see in our remaining chapters, it is personally and socially valueable in many ways. Before leaving our discussion of humor as aesthetic experience, however, I would like to respond to Miss Fidditch by saying something about the importance of humor in aesthetic education and in education generally. Then we will close by responding to Miss Fidditch's spiritual great-grandfather, Plato.

The area of aesthetic education in which the student is most often exposed to humor, as we said earlier, is the study of literature. Unfortunately, however, even when teachers admit the existence of humor in literature, they often overlook a good deal of it because they think of humor as a particular genre of literature—humorous writing is too often thought of as the kind of writing found in comedies (and in "comic relief" scenes in tragedies) and in the prose of a handful of writers like Mark Twain. With this kind of attitude a teacher will mention humor when discussing a comedy or piece by Mark Twain, but then forget about it when he or she returns to "standard, serious" writing. And yet if students were educated to read literature sensitively, they would find humor in practically every writer. The poetry of Robert Frost, for example, has been read by millions of students, but how many of them have noticed the rich humor in a good number of Frost's poems? How many teachers have assigned "A Drumlin Woodchuck," in which Frost speaks from the animal's point of view describing the precautions he takes against his enemies, particularly the careful construction of his two-door burrow? The poem ends with these lines:

And if after the hunt goes past
And the double-barreled blast
(Like war and pestilence
And the loss of common sense),

If I can with confidence say
That still for another day,
Or even another year,
I will be there for you, my dear,

It will be because, though small
As measured against the All,
I have been so instinctively thorough
About my crevice and burrow.

If teachers want every poem to have a "lesson," this one does, and it is as profound a lesson as that found in "Stopping by Woods on a Snowy Evening" or "The Road Not Taken," those standards which constitute all most students ever see of Frost's poetry. But what makes this poem so delightful is that it treats the ultimate issues of life and death with a warm sense of humor.

In another poem, "Birches," Frost uses humor to make a point about the process of poetic creation itself. He begins:

When I see birches bend to left and right
Across the lines of straighter darker trees,
I like to think some boy's been swinging them.

"But," he continues, "swinging doesn't bend them down to stay/ As ice-storms do." He then goes off on a sixteen-line tangent about ice-storms, returning abruptly with the lines:

But I was going to say when Truth broke in
With all her matter-of-fact about the ice-storm . . .

These lines are humorous because they suggest that the poet is not in control of the poem he is writing, that Truth breaks in wherever it pleases. In one sense this is a silly notion, of course, but in another it characterizes perfectly the feeling poets and artists often have that their conscious rational minds are not where their poems or art comes from.

Humor in literature, then, can give us insights into the process of writing itself, but it is valuable to the student of literature in other ways as well. Humorous writing embodies many of the qualities that are essential to good writing of any kind. Humorous writing, for instance, is writing that can shift perspective, even to the most unusual points of view. It can induce one feeling in a reader and then suddenly switch to another incompatible feeling. And to succeed in doing such things, humorous writing must pay attention to the role of each word and phrase used, to all their connotations, and to the tone they establish. The writer of humor, too, is able to play with the very words and concepts that are his medium; this also requires skill. Humorous writing, in short, is careful, versatile, imaginative writing. The more a student learns to appreciate humor in writing, therefore, the more he or she will be able to appreciate some of the basic qualities of good writing in general. And this appreciation will not only allow the student to get more out of literature, but also serve as a foundation for his or her own efforts at creative writing.

The same values of humor which we have been discussing with reference to writing are found too in the plastic arts; but if humor is merely neglected in classes on literature, it is virtually ignored in art appreciation classes. Picasso, for instance, is often discussed at great length, but the humor that animates many of his works is not even mentioned. More fortunate students will perhaps get a ten-second look at a slide of Picasso's *Bull's Head,* a sculpture cast from a bicycle seat attached vertically to the center of a set of handlebars; a few teachers may even refer to the imagination shown by Picasso in seeing a bull's head in the seat and handlebars; but rarely will a teacher mention the obvious fact that this sculpture is basically a visual joke. In the work of surrealists like Dali and Magritte we find not just visual joking but a playing around with our very sense of visual reality—with the logic of two dimensions and three dimensions, for example, or our ordinary distinctions between the solid and the fluid, the animate and the inanimate. Students would learn a lot from studying such work, especially about their own unexamined assumptions about reality and its representation in art. But artists like Dali and Magritte are usually treated merely as oddities who do not belong in a "serious" course on art.

If teachers paid more attention to humor, moreover, they would also find that it is most useful in getting students to see more aesthetically and creatively. In an introductory aesthetics course, I spend the first few classes showing slides of familiar objects and asking the students to see these objects as something other than what they are. We look at slides of the front ends of cars, for instance, and talk about them as if they were faces. Old Volkswagens, most students agree, look friendly and well-intentioned, if somewhat naive. Other cars look aristocratic and aloof. We also look at slides of chairs from different historical periods and from different contemporary schools of design. We discuss questions like "Would this chair be happy to have you sit in it?" Exercises like this are treated with humor and enthusiasm by students, most of whom seldom have a chance to exercise their imagination in a classroom. And these exercises bring home to students, far better than any theoretical lecture could, the connection between the aesthetic attitude, imagination, and play.

Much more would have to be said to give an adequate introduction to the topic of humor in aesthetic education—I have not even mentioned humor in music or dance, for example—but let's leave off here to offer a few equally sketchy comments on humor in education generally.

All the features of humor we have been discussing, especially its connection with imagination and creativity, and the flexibility of perspective which it brings, are valuable not just in aesthetic education but in all education. Unfortunately, however, many teachers see no place for humor in education. And the reason for this attitude is not hard to understand. As is obvious to anyone who has spent time in a classroom, a teacher is not someone who merely transmits a certain body of facts to a group of students. Like it or not, a teacher projects his or her attitudes toward the material being taught, toward the students, and toward the society in which they all live. A teacher, that is, projects a good deal of his or her view of the world. The reason why many teachers do not have any humor in their teaching, and indeed fear humor when it comes from their students, is that their own view of the world is relatively humorless. They don't show flexibility in their perspective on the material they teach, or in their interactions with students, because as people they are basically inflexible. They do not try to cultivate playfulness or even imagination in their students because their own attitudes toward things are neither playful nor imaginative. And so in their teaching they project a one-dimensional attitude which tells students that education, and life in general, is a serious business, consisting essentially of a series of lessons to be remembered and problems to be solved (and solved as straightforwardly as possible). Life is fundamentally doing one's job. Is it any wonder that under the tutelage of such teachers, children who come to school at age five with imagination, playfulness, and curiosity, have lost these qualities—at least in the classroom—within a year or two?

A teacher who integrates humor into the learning experience, of course, will have to put more effort into teaching. He or she will be dealing with students no longer as mere receivers of prepackaged information, but as curious, playful, creative human beings, who experiment with ideas, occasionally ask outlandish questions, and may sometimes even get bored enough to make wisecracks. Such a teacher will no longer be able to present his or her material as neat chunks of knowledge which can be understood in only one way, nor to present trains of thought which move inexorably from a given point to a pre-established conclusion. He or she will not even take it as given that all of class time must be spent in learning something.

Understandably, many teachers might be reluctant, even afraid, to allow this kind of flexibility in the learning experience. As I said, it calls for more effort on the part of the teacher; exercising control in such a multidimensional relationship, to cite but one potential problem, is more difficult than in a one-dimensional relationship. At the same time, the rewards of this kind of teaching, for both student and teacher, are incomparably greater than in the Miss Fidditch kind. And if we are genuinely interested not just in the transmission of facts and skills, but in the education of full human beings, then I think that we have no choice but to integrate humor into the learning experience.

We began this chapter with three traditional attacks on humor, and have been responding to them indirectly by arguing for the value of humor as a kind of aesthetic experience. Now it might be useful to close the chapter with a few words in more direct response to the three attacks. Plato's first charge, remember, was that in humor we are exposed to something base, which might infect us with its evil. The answer here is that the proper object of humorous amusement is incongruity, and not necessarily anything morally objectionable.

Even when we are amused at moral shortcomings, moreover, it is not clear how we are thereby tempted to imitate them. Plato's third charge, that laughter is basically scorn, was shown false in our earlier examination of the superiority theory; and numerous examples of humor that is not unsociable or uncharitable have been added in this chapter. We are left, then, with Plato's second charge that in humor we lose control of our rational faculties, and become silly, irresponsible, and less truly human. Plato makes this charge against humor because he considers amusement at humor to be a kind of emotion. I have argued elsewhere that amusement is not an emotion;[11] here, however, I simply want to argue that humor involves not a suspension of reason, but a nonserious use of reason.

Clearly, reason is necessary for humor; without it we could not even recognize incongruity, much less enjoy it or create it for enjoyment. Infants and the higher animals, which have much in common with human adults, including a capacity for emotions, lack a capacity for humor, because they lack our rationality. They can learn, they have expectations, and they can be surprised. But because they don't have our conceptual system with its class concepts, causal patterns, and so on, they don't appreciate incongruity; at most they react to the violation of their expectations with puzzlement, frustration, or distress. We, by contrast, can enjoy having our expectations violated, sometimes even when the incongruity involves our own failure, because we can look beyond the mere practical aspects of individual situations to understand the world in a *general* way, abstracted from its particular relations to ourselves.

Philosophers like Plato would give us to believe that human rationality has to reject incongruity, that it is counter to our nature to enjoy it. Santayana speaks of an "undertone of disgust" that mingles with amusement at humor, and claims that "man, being a rational animal, can like absurdity no better than he can like hunger or cold."[12] But this is to have much too narrow a picture of human rationality, to restrict it to the practical and the contemplative uses of reason. Surely we can use reason not only for inquiry and to guide our lives, but also for the occasional game of chess and even to play with our perceptions and imaginings, as in humor. Indeed, the person who was incapable of enjoying incongruity and conceptual play, who used reason only to know the world and act appropriately in each situation, would be less, not more fully human. It is the schizo-phrenic, not the fully rational person, who has no sense of humor. The medievals were clearly much closer to the truth than Plato or Santayana, when they said that it is *because* we are rational animals that we are also the animals that laugh.

# 8

# Humor and Freedom

In comparing humor with aesthetic experience generally, in the last chapter, I mentioned the liberating effect of humor as part of the reason we delight in it. In this chapter I would like to extend this observation, and connect it with the role of distancing in humor, in order to further reveal the value of humor in human life.

Perhaps the easiest place to see the liberating effect of humor is in the political sphere. The person with a sense of humor can never be fully dominated, even by a government which imprisons him, for his ability to laugh at what is incongruous in the political situation will put him above it to some extent, and will preserve a measure of his freedom—if not of movement, at least of thought. As Lord Shaftesbury wrote, in a passage cited earlier in another connection, "the natural free spirits of ingenious men, if imprisoned or controlled, will find other ways of motion to relieve themselves in their constraint; and whether it be burlesque, mimicry or buffoonery, they will be glad at any rate to vent themselves, and be revenged on their constrainers . . . 'Tis the persecuting spirit has raised the bantering one."[1]

It is because of the freedom of thought in humor, and indeed in aesthetic experience generally, that humorists and artists have traditionally been *personae non gratae* under rigidly controlled political

regimes. In Plato's *Republic*, remember, the arts were to be suppressed, with rare exceptions like certain kinds of music useful in
training the young. Laughter, too, Plato frowned upon as weakening
the character and confusing the mind. The Soviets today, of course,
keep tight controls on all the arts, making sure, as Plato advised,
that they are permitted only where they can serve the purposes of the
state. Humor, too, is controlled in the Soviet Union, at least to the
extent that this is possible. *Krokodil,* the state journal of humor, was
established by the Central Committee to carry out the following
task: "By the weapon of satire, to expose the thieves of public property, grafters, bureaucrats, boastful snobs, subservient individuals
and rottenness; to react to an international event promptly and to
subject to criticism the bourgeois culture of the West, showing its
ideological insignificance and decay." It is encouraging that the staff
of *Krokodil* has sometimes gone beyond these announced goals, and
on at least one occasion it has become necessary to replace the whole
staff. Hitler was so wary of the danger of humor to the Third Reich
that he had special "joke courts" set up for, among other things,
punishing people who named their dogs and horses "Adolph." As
Hermann Goering instructed the Academy of German Law, the
telling of a joke could be an act against the Fuehrer, against the
state, or even against the whole Nazi *Weltanschauung.*

A dictatorship requires simple blind obedience, preferably based
on hero worship, but at least on fear, of the dictator. And the spirit
of humor is incompatible with both hero worship and fear. Even the
most powerful of rulers, as the old saying goes, puts on his pants one
leg at a time.

Political humor is important, of course, not only in resisting or
coping under a dictatorship, but also in the day to day workings of a
democracy. The relatively open spirit of American political life has
in large part been due to our traditions of political cartooning and
satire. And it has been when we were afraid to joke about the
government, as in the McCarthy years, that we suffered most as a
democratic people.

Humor is liberating not only in the face of political constraints,
but also with social mores. When we look at our own culture with a
sense of humor, we see our customs, which we often take for granted
as the natural way to do things, as just one possible way of doing

things. Humor can even override moral constraints. The breaking of the rules may occur, as in jokes, merely in the imagination. Indeed, Freud thought that the main function of jokes was to allow us to express morally unacceptable desires. Or the spirit of humor may take the form of a carnival, which in many cultures involves the suspension of moral rules, particularly those governing sexual conduct.

The freedom which humor brings extends even to the constraints of logic and reason itself. The philosopher Schopenhauer, burdened more than most people, perhaps, by the constraints of reason, suggested that humor amuses us because it violates what is supposed to be inviolable—the rational order of things. "It must therefore be diverting to us," he wrote, "to see that strict, untiring, troublesome governess, the reason, for once convicted of insufficiency."[2] Lewis Carroll, the author of the Alice books and other marvellously absurd stories and poems, was in real life Charles Dodgson, a mathematician and logician; in his humorous writings he could revel in non sequiturs and other fallacies, could invent new words and change the meanings of words in midsentence, could do all the things that he was forbidden to do in his mathematical and logical work.

None of us would want to be permanent residents of a place like Wonderland. Nor would we want to give up our capacity for rational thought—without it we simply wouldn't be able to live as human beings. But we all need the occasional bout of irrationality and even silliness. If things get too understandable and too orderly, the novelty and surprise goes out of our experience; and then, even if things are going smoothly, life easily becomes "just one damn thing after another."

Another way of approaching the connection between humor and freedom is with the notion of distance mentioned earlier. When we find an incongruous situation funny, we are disengaged from doing anything in that situation. Consider the case cited in Chapter 2 of someone groggily pouring the morning coffee over the cornflakes. The person who snaps to what he is doing and breaks into laughter is for the moment detached from his action of making breakfast; he has stepped back from what he has done to enjoy its bumbling absurdity. The person who gets upset in this situation, on the other hand, who curses because of the ruined cornflakes, wasted coffee, and lost time, has not gotten any distance from the practical situation, but is still making breakfast.

Humor is valuable in giving us distance and perspective not only in situations where we are failing, but also in situations where we are succeeding. Reaching the goals we set for ourselves can often blind us to the necessity of evaluating those goals. But approaching our successes with a sense of humor keeps alive the critical spirit, and prevents us from overrating our achievements and getting an inflated sense of our own importance.

Now some incongruous situations are just too heavy with practical consequences for most people to find funny while they are in those situations, though, as we noted, in retrospect they may seem funny. But the more well developed a person's sense of humor, the wider the range of situations in which he can achieve the necessary distance to laugh. The spirit of humor, as Stephen Leacock put it, "views life, even life now, in as soft a light as we view the past."[3]

To the extent that we can achieve this distance from the practical side of any situation, we are free from being dominated by that situation. In some cases, such as during wartime, humor can become almost a prerequisite of survival. Viktor Frankl, who survived Auschwitz and Dachau and later came to incorporate humor into his psychotherapeutic techniques, said of the concentration camps: "Unexpectedly most of us were overcome by a grim sense of humor. We knew we had nothing to lose except our ridiculously naked lives. . . Humor was another of the soul's weapons in the fight for self-preservation. . . Humor more than anything else in the human make-up can afford an aloofness and an ability to rise above any situation, if only for a few seconds."[4]

Hospitals are another place where the distance provided by humor has a beneficial effect. If looked at from a practical point of view, the emergency room might seem a necessarily grim place, where there would be nothing to laugh about. But in fact this is not the case. In a paper presented at the Second International Conference on Humor, Drs. Douglas Lindsey and James Benjamin explained how humor is indispensable in the emergency room. By distancing themselves through humor from the gravity of the life and death situations they're in, physicians are able to preserve their sanity and to allow their medical skills to operate at peak efficiency. "The efficacy of humor in the emergency room is simply stated: it keeps us going." Diseases are given nicknames—spinal meningitis may be called "smilin' mighty Jesus," or uterine fibroids "King Neptune's fireballs." Most often the joking will be between physicians, but sometimes it may be appropriate for the doctor to joke with the patient. And sometimes humor will arise unintentionally in the treatment of the patient. Dr. Lindsey cites such a case:

> . . . the young man [was] brought in with a bullet hole over his heart, [was] admitted in coma, and promptly died. I picked up a scalpel, opened his chest from here to here, put my finger over the hole, and squeezed his heart a few times. It started. So off we go to the operating room, with me walking along one hand in the chest. On the way he woke up, raised his head to see what was going on, comprehended what he saw, and made a remark of high pertinence: "My blood type is A positive." Whereupon the efficient nurse broke in with: "Hey, Jack, before you go back to sleep would you sign the operative permit?" Which he did. In medical circles this is known as "informed consent."[5]

If humor involves a distancing from life's troubles, then perhaps the highest form of this "stepping back" is gallows humor, in which a person is able to achieve enough distance from his own situation of impending death to joke about it. When most states still had the death penalty, a prison warden told of one man who had spent his last dollar on legal advice and law books, in the hope of finding some loophole to save him from being executed. When all his efforts had failed and he was being led out of his cell to face the electric chair, he gave the warden instructions for disposing of his few remaining possessions. "And give those law books to somebody who needs 'em," he said, "give 'em to my lawyer."

The humorous attitude now begins to sound like what has traditionally been called the "philosophical attitude," and indeed the comparison is enlightening. The person who looks at his life philosophically does not let his emotions color his view; he is distanced, as we have been saying, from the practical aspects of his situation. And this calmness makes his assessment of his situation more objective, more like that of an unbiased observer. In both respects the humorous attitude is like the philosophical: the person who can appreciate the humor in his own situation is liberated from the dominance of his emotions, and so he has a more objective view of himself.

When the person with a sense of humor laughs in the face of his own failure, he is showing that his perspective transcends the particular situation he's in, and that he does not have an egocentric, overly precious view of his own endeavors. This is not to say that he lacks self-esteem—quite the contrary. It is because he feels good about himself at a fundamental level that this or that setback is not threatening to him. The person without real self-esteem, on the other hand, who is unsure of his own worth, tends to invest his whole sense of himself in each of his projects. Whether he fails or succeeds, he is not likely to see things in an objective way; because his ego rides on each of the goals he sets for himself, any failure will constitute personal defeat and any success personal triumph. He simply cannot afford to laugh at himself, whatever happens. So having a sense of humor about oneself is psychologically healthy. As A. Penjon so nicely said, it "frees us from vanity, on the one hand, and from pessimism on the other by keeping us larger than what we do, and greater than what can happen to us."[6]

Humor, then, is not only valuable in human life, but valuable in a way nothing else is. Indeed, I think it no exaggeration to claim that humor is essential to maintaining a healthy outlook on things.

People with severe mental problems usually lack a sense of humor, and, we should note, a capacity for aesthetic experience generally, because they cannot achieve any distance from the immediate practical concerns of the situation they're in. An extremely paranoid person, for example, might not find even the bowling ball in the refrigerator funny, because he might see it as part of an elaborate plot against him. Someone who views everything as having a practical relationship to himself will not be able to view things from any distance, and thus will not be able to enjoy anything simply as funny. This lack of a capacity for distance often shows up, too, in a person's inability to pretend that the world is other than as he perceives it, or even to imagine it as other than he perceives it. When a schizophrenic is asked, "What would you do if you had wings?" the typical reply is, "But I *don't* have wings." For such a person there is no possibility of looking at things as other than as they now seem to be; much like an animal, he is trapped in the world as he actually perceives it. And with this loss of the freedom of imagination there is a loss of capacity for humor and for aesthetic experience generally.

When people are working through their mental problems it is a good sign when they become able to laugh about their situation, because this shows that they are now able to look at their problems from a distance instead of from a position locked inside those problems. To the extent that we can laugh about something we have achieved a measure of objectivity about it, and this change of stance makes a big difference in the way we see things. Some psychiatrists have even developed therapeutic techniques based on this insight. One of these, Viktor Frankl calls "paradoxical therapy."[7] When a patient is overwhelmed by some problem so that he cannot get an objective view of it, Frankl tries to exaggerate the problem in the patient's eyes to the point where it seems funny to him. If the person is feeling anxious about something, for example, Frankl will tell him that of course his anxiety is well-founded—in fact, things are far worse than he thought. The repetition of such hyperbole eventually makes the person laugh at the situation that had provoked his anxiety; in so doing he gets some distance on his problem and can begin working toward a solution. Another psychiatrist who uses "paradoxical therapy" tells anxious patients to set aside a certain time of the day to be especially anxious. When that times comes and the person tries to be anxious, he feels silly, can't become anxious, and relaxes. This kind of treatment has been successful with a number of different problems, among them depression, insomnia, self-doubting, chronic complaining, sexual difficulties, jealousy, and fear.[8]

In this regard it is interesting to note that humor is one of the best weapons against the procedure known as "brainwashing." The person trying to brainwash another is essentially trying to take away that person's mental flexibility and capacity to think for himself, and implant in the person a single line of thought from which he will not deviate. But if the person can maintain his sense of humor, this will not happen. As psychiatrist William Sargent reported, based on his experience with people in concentration camps, if at any point in the brainwashing procedure the subject laughs, "the whole process is wrecked and must be begun all over again."[9]

If, as I have been urging, humor plays a key role in "mental health," it is also important to physical health. Kant and others have suggested that the movements of the lungs and other internal organs in laughter are themselves beneficial, like a massage perhaps, and that the physical gratification we feel in laughing furthers our sense of bodily well-being.[10] But the connection between humor and health runs far deeper than this. Medical research is finding more and more ways in which our thoughts, emotions, and general outlook on things influence organic processes throughout the body. The person who experiences a lot of frustration and stress on the job, as we all know, shows greater muscle tension, and often suffers from headaches, high blood pressure, and ulcers. Because humor allows us to cope better with stressful situations, it can markedly reduce tension and these other accompaniments of stress. The two emotions specifically associated with heart attacks—fear and anger—are incompatible with humor, as we have seen. And the person who has a sense of humor is not just more relaxed in the face of potentially stressful situations, but is more flexible in his approach to any situation. Even when there is not a lot going on in his environment, his imagination and innovativeness will help keep him out of a mental rut, will allow him to enjoy himself, and so will prevent boredom and depression. He will, in short, have greater internal resources for being happy than the person who lacks a sense of humor; and this is likely to manifest itself in greater physical well-being.

Though the medical benefits of humor are only now being studied in any detail, moreover,[11] there are some interesting cases that suggest that humor is not only healthy, but has actual healing power. The most famous recent case is that of Norman Cousins, the former editor of *Saturday Review*. On returning from an exhausting trip to the Soviet Union in 1964, Cousins fell sick with a serious collagen disease—the connective tissue in his spine and joints was disintegrating. The pain was intense and the prognosis discouraging; he was given only a 1-in-500 chance of fully recovering. Indeed, he was told that the disease was potentially life-threatening.

Refusing to accept this grim prognosis, Cousins took charge of his own treatment. He remembered reading that imbalances in the endocrine system often contributed to arthritis and similar diseases, and that such imbalances could be caused by negative emotions, such as he had been feeling for some time. If negative emotions were in part behind his condition, he reasoned, then perhaps he could cure himself by changing things so that he felt positive emotions.

Cousins checked out of the hospital and into a hotel, where he began his own form of humor therapy. He surrounded himself with humor books, and from his friend Allen Funt, producer of the television program, "Candid Camera," he got some of that show's funniest segments. Within a short time he found that hearty laughter had an analgesic effect—ten minutes of it would allow him to sleep without pain for a few hours. When he awoke and felt pain again, he turned the films back on. After a week of this therapy, he found that he could move his thumbs without pain. And as the weeks went by, his condition improved further; his doctors found that the connective tissue in his joints was regenerating. A short time later he was able to go back to work full time, and though it took years for his condition to fully reverse itself, he knew that, thanks to his humor therapy, he was recovering.

Researchers have begun to study other possible ways in which a sense of humor contributes to one's health. It may well be, for example, that people with a better sense of humor tend to live longer. But whatever details we discover in years to come, I think that it is incontrovertible that humor has psychological and physical benefits that make it an important part of our lives. Wittgenstein said that "the world of the happy man is a different one from that of the unhappy man." (*Tractatus* 6.43.) Somewhat less elegantly, I think we can say that the world of the person with a sense of humor is a different world from that of the person without one.

All our talk of the benefits of humor may have made it sound as though humor is always a good thing, but as we saw in Chapter 2 in our examination of cruel and derisive humor, this is not the case. Before ending this chapter, then, we might say something about ethical limitations on humor. And the notion of practical disengagement we have been using provides a helpful way of understanding these limitations.

To find some situation funny, as we have seen, is to enjoy the incongruity in it. And to enjoy the incongruity in a situation, we need to be without urgent practical concerns; we need to be practically disengaged from what is taking place. If we see a situation as incongruous but also as dangerous to us, then we won't be amused; instead we'll be concerned with the practical aspects of the situation, and we may well feel fear. Instead of enjoying the situation, we'll be thinking of ways to escape it. Similarly, if an incongruous situation involves another person's suffering, we may feel pity and not amusement; instead of enjoying the situation we may be thinking of ways to alleviate the suffering. So too, anger, resentment, and other negative emotions can block our enjoyment of an incongruous situation and lead us to act to change or escape that situation instead.

Now if we ask what kinds of situations people are in fact capable of finding humorous, I think the answer is that any incongruity whatever might amuse someone. As history shows, even the most horrible disasters and atrocities have amused at least a few people. But if we adopt a moral point of view and ask what kinds of situations people should be able to find funny, we will rule out in the answer those situations which people should not, as moral agents, be able to disengage themselves practically from and simply enjoy.

The most common kind of morally inappropriate humor is probably that in which someone laughs at another's misfortune, when that misfortune is so great that it should evoke the laugher's sympathy and practical concern instead. If you have bumped your head very lightly on a door, say, I may find that amusing, and indeed you may laugh yourself. But if you have been struck by a car, then I should not be able to get sufficient distance from your injury and suffering to laugh. This kind of incongruity should instead engage my practical concern: I should feel sympathy and be thinking of ways to help you. To laugh in such a situation would be to show a callousness that was morally reprehensible. It is this moral insight that is behind the traditional maxim of Aristotle, Cicero, and others, that we laugh only at the minor misfortunes of others. As a claim about what people do in fact laugh at, it is false. But as a prescription for what they should not laugh at, it is sound.

In creating humor, too, it is morally acceptable to cause minor inconvenience or discomfort for the sake of a laugh, but not major inconvenience or intense pain. In playing practical jokes, for example, a safe rule of thumb is that the person who is on the receiving end of the joke should be able to laugh too. A flower that squirts water is acceptable; one that squirted sulfuric acid would not be.

Now someone might be prepared to accept my idea of an ethically objectionable practical joke here but not my idea that being amused can sometimes be morally objectionable. In playing a practical joke, after all, we are *doing* something, and we are morally responsible for our actions, here actions that cause needless suffering or inconvenience. But in being amused we are not doing anything. Amusement, like other forms of enjoyment and like emotions, it can be argued, is an involuntary response to a situation, something that happens to us rather than something which we do. Can we be any more morally responsible for our amusement than for, say, our enjoying the taste of avocado or our feeling fear?

The claim here that amusement is not an action is, of course, beyond challenge. But it does not follow that we can not be morally responsible for our amusement. Though not an action, amusement is often under our control, and we can justifiably be held responsible for what we can control.[12] In this respect amusement is like emotions, which, though they are not actions, are sometimes under our control, and so sometimes among the things for which we can be held responsible. We are sometimes blamed for feeling anger, for example, in inappropriate circumstances—not just for expressing our anger in actions but for allowing ourselves to "get so worked up over such a little thing." And such blame is appropriate if we could have prevented our anger by some action, such as leaving the sitation or counting aloud to ten, or by some nonbehavioral means such as reasoning with ourselves. Other negative emotions like hatred, resentment, and jealousy, can be controlled in similar ways.

Our ability to control our emotions goes beyond our minimizing or preventing inappropriate emotions, furthermore; sometimes we can bring about emotions appropriate to a particular situation. Pity is a good example here, and the one most relevant to our discussion of controlling amusement. If we witness someone's suffering and yet find ourselves initially unmoved by it, we may recognize that something is amiss. Here we may create sympathy and pity in ourselves by focusing our attention on the details of the person's suffering and its undeserved nature, perhaps comparing it to suffering we have experienced, and even talking out the situation with ourselves.

We control amusement in much the same way we control emotions. This control will often involve both the creation of pity and the prevention of enjoyment of the incongruity involved; indeed the two go hand in hand. If we are in a situation where there is an incongruity involving great suffering, and we find ourselves beginning to be amused, we might block this callous amusement by directing our thoughts to the suffering involved so that we feel pity instead of amusement for what has happened to the person. Sometimes, of course, we will not have this control over our amusement; but even then, we may be able to suppress the expression of our amusement, or if necessary, even leave the situation so that our insensitivity won't aggravate the person's suffering.

None of what has been said here should be taken to imply that it is always wrong to enjoy or even to instigate humor that offends people. While we should not hurt innocent people with our humor, some people, such as dictators, have no claim on us not to joke about them or engage in outright ridicule. Jokes about Hitler, for example, gave those he was oppressing some feeling of freedom and kept alive a morally praiseworthy resistance to his regime. On a smaller scale, we might use humor to embarrass a person who is acting out of bigotry, in order to wake him up to what he is doing, and to give support to the people he is mistreating.

So far we have been considering the ethical dimensions of enjoying incongruity in certain situations where suffering is involved; but the topic of ridicule reminds us that sometimes our laughter expresses both our enjoyment of some incongruity and also our enjoyment of another's suffering, failure, or debasement itself, as in hostile or cruel humor. As we saw earlier, though, the latter kind of enjoyment is not essential to humor, nor is it found only in humor. We may enjoy incongruity by itself, that is, and we may enjoy another's suffering, failure, or debasement by itself. (Where there is no enjoyment of incongruity, as in pure scorn or cruelty, there is not humor, even if there is laughter.) An ethical examination of cases of humor which involve this kind of enjoyment not essential to humor, would involve a broader treatment of the enjoyment of other people's misfortune generally. Such an examination is beyond the scope of our present discussion: we might say here simply that cases of humor involving scorn, hostility, and cruelty, would come under an ethics of scorn, hostility, and cruelty generally. Where it is ethically objectionable in general to allow ourselves to enjoy another's suffering, failure, or debasement, it is ethically objection-able to allow ourselves to enjoy such things *along with* the enjoyment of incongruity.

I have been discussing the moral appropriateness of laughing at another person's situation, but before closing this discussion of the ethics of humor, I should add that it can also be morally inappropri-ate to laugh about one's own situation, if by doing so we are detach-ing ourselves from our own moral responsibilities. The person who habitually drives while drunk, for example, may joke about not re-membering how he got home, or even about near accidents, as a way of not facing the wrongness of his actions and his need to change. The principle here is the same as before: there are some things we should not disengage ourselves from. If a situation requires our con-cern and action, we should not treat that situation as humorous as a way of shirking our moral responsibilities.

Humor, then, is a powerful force for liberation in our lives, and is clearly a boon to the human race. Indeed, the person who shares humor with others, especially in times of trouble, can be looked upon as a doer of good works. But as we have seen, there are times when humor can disengage us from what should be our moral con-cerns, and then it is not appropriate. To be able to stand back and laugh at things is one of the most valuable traits of our species; still, this is not a proper reaction in every situation.

# 9

# The Social Value of Humor

In considering the value of humor so far, we have concentrated on the individual person. To get a full picture of the value of humor, however, we need to look at how it functions socially. Humor is primarily a social phenomenon, as are other forms of human enjoyment. We rarely laugh when alone, even at things that would evoke our laughter if we were with others. And if we are in a group and find that we are the only one laughing at something, we will usually cover our mouth and stifle our laughter, at least until others join in. This social aspect of laughter shows, too, in its contagiousness. Group laughter tends to work like atomic fission. Your laughter makes me laugh harder, and mine in turn reinforces your laughter. Indeed, sometimes another person's laughing is enough to get us started, even though we don't know what is making him laugh. Comedians and theater owners have long been aware that it is much easier to get a full house laughing than just half a house, especially if the smaller crowd is spread out so that they don't reinforce one anothers' laughter. It is because of the contagious nature of laughter, too, that television comedies often use "laugh tracks."

Perhaps the most extreme manifestation of the contagiousness of laughter is the "laughter epidemic" in which large numbers of people are made to laugh convulsively not by any organic cause but just by the laughter of the others. The most famous of these epidemics occurred in Africa in the mid-1960s. It started among girls at a Catholic high school, who "gave" it to their mothers and sisters when they went home. Their laughter, often mixed with heavy sobbing, lasted from a few hours to more than two weeks, and usually prevented them from eating. Many "victims" collapsed from exhaustion. Over a thousand women and girls were affected, and the epidemic lasted two months.[1]

Laughter is not only contagious, but in spreading from person to person, it has a cohesive effect. Laughing together unites people. Those who hold the superiority theory of laughter often point to the fact that groups unite in laughter against outsiders as evidence for their theory. But ridicule is not the only kind of group laughter that has a binding effect. To laugh with another person for whatever reason, even if only at a piece of absurdity, is to get closer to that person. Indeed, humor can even be directed at the laughers themselves, and still have this unifying effect. Getting stuck in an elevator between floors with people, or running into people at the bank door on a bank holiday, often makes us laugh at our common predicament, and this laughter brings us together.

When two people are quarreling, one of the first things they stop doing together is laughing; they refuse to laugh at each other's attempts at humor, and refuse to laugh together at something incongruous happening to them. As soon as they begin to laugh once more, we know that the end of the quarrel is at hand.

The cohesive effect of humor is connected with its ability to distance us from the practical aspects of the situation we're in, and with the shared enjoyment which it involves. To joke with others is to put aside practical considerations for the moment, and doing this tends to make everyone relax. Sharing humor is in this respect like sharing an enjoyable meal. It is precisely because the quarrelers do not want to put aside practical considerations and do not want to relax together, that they will not respond to each other's attempts at humor (if, indeed, any are made). Similarly, people who are quarreling often refuse to eat together.

Sharing humor with others, then, is a friendly social gesture. It shows our acceptance of them and our desire to please them. When we are anxious about meeting someone because we're not sure how that person will react to us, the first laugh we share (if it occurs) will be important, for it will mark the other person's acceptance of us. We often start off converstaions with new acquaintances with a small joke, of course, for just this reason—to set up the mood of acceptance and make the other person relax. And public speakers have for centuries begun speeches with a joke for the same reason.

The person with a sense of humor, even in practical situations, is likely to interact with others more smoothly than the humorless person. As we saw earlier, someone with a sense of humor is more imaginative and flexible in his general outlook, and so is less likely to get obsessed with any particular issue or approach to an issue. Such a person will be more open to suggestions from others, and so will be more approachable. The fact that a sense of humor keeps one from getting too self-centered or defensive abut his ego also helps in this regard.

Humor also facilitates social interaction in a number of situations where it is added to a basically serious piece of communication to eliminate the offensiveness which that communication might otherwise have. When we have a complaint to make to a friend, for example, we often do so with a jocular gripe. By making our complaint amusing, we show the person that the problem is not of overwhelming importance and that we have maintained our perspective on it—"It's not the end of the world," as we sometimes say. And our humor not only shows that we have some distance from the problem, but it also tends to allow our friend some distance. He isn't put on the spot and forced to defend himself in the way that people often are when their actions are criticized in a serious tone. By using the jocular gripe we don't set up a confrontation; rather we invite the person to step back and laugh with us. The tension often associated with serious criticism is thus reduced and the person is more likely to consider the reasonableness of the complaint. Indeed, most people seem able to take almost any criticism from a friend if it is expressed in a humorous way.

Humor serves to create distance and smooth out social interaction not just in making complaints, of course, but in asking potentially offensive questions, admitting to blunders, accepting praise graciously, and in many other interchanges. As we saw in the last chapter, too, humor may also be used in social interaction in morally objectionable ways. People may "laugh off" comments about their serious wrongdoings as a way of shirking moral responsibility. They may use humor and laughter as a way of ingratiating themselves with their superiors. Humor may even be used to exert an unfair kind of pressure on someone to do something he doesn't want to do: he wants to say no, but the request is laden with such "friendly" humor that he'll seem like a "poor sport" if he doesn't comply.

Even when humor is used (or abused) for some end other than simply amusing another person, we should note, humor for that other person can still be an end in itself. If we present humor to someone to make him like us, for example, *he* does not enjoy the humor as a means to achieving some further goal, even though *we* have an ulterior motive. He simply enjoys it. Humor is like other aesthetic objects in this respect. If I give you a piece of sculpture so that you'll owe me a favor, that doesn't destroy the self-contained-ness of your aesthetic enjoyment of that sculpture.

We enjoy humor the most, perhaps, when we feel that it is offered with no ulterior motive—not even the altruistic one of getting us to relax. We want the other person simply to amuse us, with no strings attached. This is the kind of humor found among close friends. Indeed, the frequency of nonmanipulative humor in a group's interaction is a good indicator of the the intimacy of the group. We can usually determine who someone's best friends are by determining whom he enjoys humor with the most—people who talked for hours without any humorous interchange by all odds just couldn't be close friends.

In many ways the sharing of humor in a group is like the sharing of a meal, or any other pleasurable experience. But humor, because it requires no specific setting or equipment, is especially versatile as a form of enjoyable interchange. And unlike, say, listening to a concert together, humor is not just passive but calls for imagination and creativity from its participants. Humor is versatile, too, in that it mixes so well with other kinds of conversation. Friends often share a good deal of their daily experience, and so in a conversation there may be little new information that they are able to give one another. But making a funny comment doesn't require any new information; it requires only a new way of looking at things which everyone may already know about. People who have a common store of experience may be unable to inform each other, but they can always amuse each other, by playing with the reality which they have in common. In many conversations, indeed, imaginative humor is valued more than information.

In humorous conversation we may play not just with reality outside the conversation, but also with the very moves of conversation itself. We can get a humorous effect, as we saw in Chapter 6, by playfully violating the conventions governing serious conversation. Instead of saying what we believe, and uttering sentences of warning and criticism sincerely, for example, we may engage in kidding—mock claims, mock warning, and mock criticism. Kidding is funny and enjoyable because we are taking forms of speech intended for serious communication and discarding the serious purpose. Like mock physical fighting, mock criticism can be enjoyed by both parties because they know it is only play. Indeed, it can even be an expression of affection, as in the "roast," the banquet where someone's friends take turns at giving speeches full of wisecracks about him.

Human beings seem to have a basic need for playing, not just with the conventions of conversation, but with all conventions.[2] As a species we need customs to structure and regulate our relationships, of course, but we seem to have just as strong a need to occasionally let our hair down and act silly with one another. For thousands of years we have even institutionalized silly action with festivals where the ordinary rules are temporarily suspended. At least as far back as the ancient Egyptians, the courts of pharoahs and kings have had their jesters, whose job it was to introduce playful silliness into the ruler's otherwise serious day. In most cases, court jesters were even allowed to make fun of the king. Among the American Indians of the Southwest, tribal clowns formed a priestly class, and in their ritual clowning were allowed to say or do almost anything, including the breaking of sexual taboos.

In Western cultures, of course, institutionalized silliness has had a long history. The Greeks and Romans had festivals tied to the seasons, which were a time for breaking loose and acting foolishly. All kinds of sexual activity were allowed, in part because these festivals were based on fertility rites. Clowning and fertility go together, some have suggested, in that both overcome the individual's suffering and death.[3] In medieval Christian Europe we find a "Feast of

Fools"; modeled on liturgical feats, it included such things as replacing the usual vespers for the day with a mixture of all the vespers throughout the year. Wilder abuses also took place, and the Feast of Fools was eventually suppressed by the Council of Basel in 1435. Nonetheless, much of it survived and traces can be found even today in Mardi Gras celebrations.

The intellectual ferment of the fifteenth and sixteenth centuries produced a heightened appreciation of the value of humor and silliness, especially as an antidote to blind allegiance or orthodoxy. In sixteenth-century Poland a "fool society" called the Babinian Republic was established. When nonmembers did something sufficiently foolish, they were invited to join, by assuming an office appropriate to what they had done. One could be made an archbishop, for example, for speaking publicly on issues about which he was ignorant. The society soon grew to include almost every important church and government official in the country. When the King of Poland asked if the Babinian Republic also had a king, he was told that as long as he was alive the society would not dream of electing another.[4]

A better known example of the "fool movement" of this period was Erasmus's *In Praise of Folly,* a book which so nicely captures the social value of humor and silliness, that we might cite its central argument as a fitting conclusion to this chapter. The work is a long speech made by the goddess Folly on her own behalf. She argues that it is foolishness and not the calculations of reason that makes possible everything we treasure most in life. It is folly, especially, that allows us to live together and even love one another. To have a friend or spouse we have to have a sense of humor and foolishly overlook that person's faults; a rational assessment of what a friendship or marriage was going to involve would keep us aloof from the rest of our species. Even to have a good opinion of ourselves, without which no one else would love us, we need a foolish, unrealistic self-image.

The completely rational and realistic person, Dame Folly suggests, would love neither himself nor anyone else; indeed he would probably despair and kill himself.

> In sum, no society, no union in life, could be either pleasant or lasting without me [Folly]. A people does not for long tolerate its prince, or a master tolerate his servant, a handmaiden her mistress, a teacher his

student, a friend his friend, a wife her husband, a landlord his tenant, a partner his partner, or a boarder his fellow-boarder, except as they mutually or by turns are mistaken, on occasion flatter, on occasion wisely wink, and otherwise soothe themselves with the sweetness of folly.[5]

# 10
# Humor and Life

O<small>UR</small> exploration of the personal and social value of humor has shown humor to be much more than just an experience in this or that situation; it can be, as Stephen Leacock said, "a part of the interpretation of life."[1] Having a sense of humor doesn't simply provide us with occasional moments of refreshment in life's struggles, but gives us an approach to life as a whole. It is this widest value of humor that I would like to examine in this final chapter.

A useful way to understand the humorous attitude, whether toward some particular situation or toward life generally, is to contrast it with the serious attitude. When we say that a person's attitude toward something is a serious one, we mean that he considers it important, and that his intentions toward it, as well as the way he thinks and speaks about it, are earnest. Someone who is serious about a political cause, for example, will have a strong desire that it succeed, will devote lots of time and effort to it, and will not speak about it flippantly. To have a serious attitude toward something is to believe it worthy of our resolute attention, and to allow it to make demands on us. We believe that something important is at stake, and that our action will make a difference.

The person who is serious about something tends to be single-minded regarding it, both in having a wholehearted devotion to it, and in not countenancing other evaluations of it. He will probably be solemn when discussing it, and will not even allow others to treat it lightly.

All this contrasts sharply with the humorous attitude. To have a humorous attitude toward some issue is to be distanced from its practical aspects. The situation we find funny does not have an urgency about it for us; it does not command our practical attention. Rather than feeling governed by the situation and obliged to look at it in only one way, we feel playful toward it and thus ourselves in control. We can look at things in unusual ways and see amusing similarities between them; we can make false or preposterous statements; we can feign attitudes toward things—all for fun.

To have a serious attitude or a humorous attitude toward life in general is to approach most of the situations one faces in one of the two ways we've been describing. The fundamentally serious person approaches his daily life in a practical frame of mind, expecting most situations to make important demands on him. When incongruities arise, he usually sees them as disturbances in the practical order of things—something isn't working as it should, here is another problem to be solved. The person who has a humorous attitude toward life, on the other hand, has the capacity for distancing himself from the practical aspects of most situations, and simply enjoying the many incongruities he experiences or thinks up.

The emotional lives of these two kinds of person are going to be different, too. While the serious person tends to be solemn and anxious about how things are going to turn out, the person with a rich sense of humor tends to be more relaxed, less disappointed by failure, and in general more cheerful.

These two will also have different attitudes toward the proper place of amusement in human life. The serious person will see little place for amusement, and even where he admits its appropriateness will treat it as a way of refreshing himself for more serious activity. As Aristotle put it, we should amuse ourselves only for the sake of being serious.[2] For the person with a humorous outlook, however, amusement is valuable not only as a means but as an end, just as any aesthetic experience is, and as Aristotle argued that philosophical contemplation was. He will not only be amused more often than the serious person, but will enjoy moments of amusement for their own sake. Such a person will often have practical concerns, of course, and will work as well as play. And yet he will not get locked into a practical frame of mind—even while working he will retain his ability to occasionally step back and laugh at the incongruities which we all encounter every day.

Having a sense of humor, then, involves a flexibility and openness to experience which a fundamentally serious person lacks. In part this flexibility comes from the realization that what is important is relative to the situation someone is in and to his point of view. Nothing is important *simpliciter*. What calls for practical concern under one set of circumstances would not under different circumstances, or even if looked at from a different point of view. Having one's pants rip, for example, might be a matter of great concern if one is on the way to a meeting at the White House, but at a party with friends such an event will probably be cause for good-natured laughter all around. Similarly, the destruction of one's car would under ordinary circumstances be cause for alarm, but in a severe flood where people are happy just to be escaping with their lives, it might be of no concern—indeed, it might be funny—to see one's car floating away. One of the reasons many city people enjoy camping, mountain climbing, and other forms of "roughing it," is that these activities cause a shift in their perspective on what is important and what is not important. Out in the woods, gains and declines in the stock market, which might ordinarily be one's prime concern, can suddenly become of no interest. And things normally taken for granted, such as where tonight's food is coming from and where one is going to sleep, can become major concerns.

A nice dramatization of this relativity of values is found in George Pal's 1951 science fiction movie *When Worlds Collide.* At the beginning we see a courier pilot whose primary value seems to be making money. But when a packet he is delivering to a group of astronomers reveals that within a few months a star is going to collide with Earth, everything changes. Suddenly money becomes unimportant to him; he starts laughingly lighting his cigarettes with $20 bills.

A group of scientists set out to build a rocket ship that will get a few people off the doomed Earth to a new planet, and in the course of this work everything else becomes unimportant. One wealthy industrialist who had been very concerned with money and power liquidates his holdings to help finance the rocket, that his own life might be spared. Two other industrialists finance the mission to save not themselves but a few representatives of the human race. The middle-aged scientist who heads the project gives up his seat on the rocket ship at the last minute in order to lighten the load—the new planet, he says, is not for him but for the young. In the "big picture" he now sees his own life as unimportant.

We could even imagine this story taking a different twist: suppose that in testing the rocket the scientists discovered that it was not going to work, so that *everyone* faced extinction within a few days. In that situation everything would lose its urgency. It would be relatively easy to distance oneself from practical considerations, and laugh at any incongruity, since nothing that anyone did would make much of a difference. We might even imagine someone sufficiently distant from what was going on, that when the planet Earth met its demise he found that funny.

And we don't have to imagine ourselves at the end of the world to appreciate the relativity of all our values, and the possible humor in anything that happens. If we simply shift to a more cosmic perspective than we usually adopt, then not only our present concerns but the whole history of our species looks insignificant.[3] Even our intellect, which sets us apart from the rest of creation and has issued in our science, our art, and our culture, is a fleeting phenomenon. Nietzsche expressed all of this nicely:

> In some remote corner of the universe, effused into innumerable solar-systems, there was once a star upon which clever animals invented cognition. It was the haughtiest . . . moment in the history of this world, but yet only a moment. After Nature had taken breath awhile the star congealed and the clever animals had to die. . . There were eternities during which this intellect did not exist, and when it has once more passed away there will be nothing to show that it has existed.[4]

Looked at from the right perspective, then, what is ordinarily important looks unimportant, and any incongruity can be funny. Indeed, this relativity itself gives a humorous cast to our lives as a whole. The ultimate humor arises, as Stephen Leacock said, from "the incongruous contrast between the eager fret of our life and its final nothingness."[5] The human condition itself is funny.

All this is not to say that the person with a sense of humor will find nothing important in life and will never have practical concerns. But he will live with the awareness that nothing is important in an absolute way; to become obsessed with something he values, or to get locked into a particular way of looking at things, he will see as unhealthy. Even when engaged in some practical task, moreover, he realizes that it is often best to take a somewhat playful and humorous attitude toward what he is doing, for the simple psychological reason that the distance of humor will keep him calm and thus working more effectively. An anxious or solemn attitude, as we said earlier in discussing humor in the emergency room, is often counterproductive.

A good example of the serious attitude toward life, with which we may contrast the humorous attitude, is found in traditional Christianity. For the Christian, of course, there *is* something supremely and absolutely important—the infinite God and our relationship to him. Because God has created everything in our world, and has a purpose for everything, too, each thing that exists and each event has a theological dimension. We are related to God not just in moments of worship, but in everything we think, say, and do. At any particular moment either we are carrying out the will of God or we are not; we are furthering his grand design for the universe, or we are working against it. Our happiness or unhappiness in this life and, more importantly, in the unending life to come, depends on whether we align our wills with the divine will. Everything we think, say, and do brings us closer either to eternal happiness or to eternal damnation. As Jesus reminded his disciples, "For every idle word you will be held accountable."

In such a picture, needless to say, human life is as serious an activity as anything could be. The will of God is an absolute standard for every aspect of our lives. There is no "time out" in which we live outside the Creator–creature relationship; everything we do has theological and therefore practical consequences. To take up the Christian stance wholeheartedly, then, is to live single-mindedly— the non-Christian might say "obsessively"—with the purpose of fulfilling the will of God.

Now few Christians may live their lives with this degree of seriousness, but that's merely because they fall short of a wholehearted commitment to Christianity. If Christians heeded the words of their Bible, they would undoubtedly be more solemn in everything they do. Activities for mere amusement would be suppressed or eliminated, and it is hard to see how laughter might survive. "A fool lifts up his voice with laughter," as we read in Ecclesiastes, "but a wise man scarcely smiles a little." If Jesus is to be our model, then there seems no place for humor in our lives. Judging from the Gospels, Jesus' attitude toward life was uniformly serious. He is never spoken of as laughing. The closest he comes to anything like humor is his wit directed against the Pharisees and Saducees, but this is sarcasm intended to embarrass or correct, not to amuse.[6]

It is no accident that Jesus is portrayed in the Gospels as having no sense of humor. His message, as we've said, is an urgent one, involving the heaviest of consequences for the whole human race. His divinity, too, would make him a completely serious person, for the Christian God could have no sense of humor. He knows fully every thing and every event in the past, present, and future, and so nothing that happened could surprise him. He could not discover something he did not already know about, nor could he adopt a new way of looking at anything. For these reasons, and because he is a changeless being, nothing that happened could amuse God; he could not experience the psychological shift that is behind laughter. He would *recognize* incongruities, but as the failures of things to be what he intended them to be—not as events which delight by jolting one's picture of the world, but as violations of his divine plan for the world. All this explains why, as Baudelaire reminds us, "the Incarnate Word was never known to laugh. For Him who knows all things, whose powers are infinite, the comic does not exist."[7]

There are many non-Christian religions which do not involve the seriousness of Christianity. Greek and Roman polytheism, for example, which had no omniscient, omnipotent creator, but only limited gods made in man's image, saw only part of human life as having a religious dimension. No one's eternal happiness rode on everything he thought, said, or did. Because there was no creator and no divine plan for everything, it was not necessary to align one's will with that of any deity; indeed, different gods had different wills. So no single way of looking at the world was required. In this kind of religion, to be sure, there will be times when seriousness is called for, but there will also be plenty of room for laughter. Indeed, Mt.

Olympus itself, we are told, often thundered with the laughter of the gods.

In a religion like Buddhism which dispenses with the notion of gods and which encourages a disengagement from the practical orientation to life, the sense of urgency found in Christianity is replaced by a flexible attitude toward experience. Indeed, awareness itself may be treated as play, as in this passage from *The Natural Freedom of the Mind,* by Long-Chen-pa, the fourteenth-century Tibetan Buddhist lama:

> Since Mind-as-such—pure from the beginning and with no root to hold to something other than itself—has nothing to do with an agent or something to be done, one's mind may well be happy. Since intrinsic awareness with no objective reference whatsoever, has no intention as to this or that, one may well be full of love toward all. Since vision and attention to the vision are not disrupted nor falling into contraries, having nothing to do with acceptance or fear, high or low, one may well be joyous. Since enactment and goal, having nothing to do with acceptance and rejection, expectation and anxiety, are not seen as something to be obtained or missed, one may well feel an inner warmth. Since everything is but an apparition perfect in being what it is, having nothing to do with good or bad, acceptance or rejection, one may well burst out in laughter.[8]

If not all religions impose a serious view of life, neither is it only religions that do so. In recent times we've seen political movements like Chinese communism that involve people so totally that they think of every aspect of their lives in rigid political categories. Similarly, one can make an absolute value out of doing one's work, achieving power, amassing wealth, learning, art, or even the pursuit of pleasure. In each case, one subordinates one's life to achieving a single goal, so that all of life becomes serious.

In contrast to any serious view of life is the humorous view, in which nothing is of absolute importance, and nothing monopolizes our attention. The world is seen as a place not only for practical activity, but also for play. Not all situations have practical significance—there are many free moments simply to be enjoyed.

Once we give up the idea that everything is related practically to us, too, we are no longer bound to seeing things in just one way. Even fanciful or downright silly perspectives are acceptable. And, as we have seen, this mental flexibility brings an openness to experience. With a sense of humor, we are not likely to become obsessed with anything or fanatic about any cause.

The nonpractical stance in humor, along with its openness to novelty in experience, keeps us from anxiety. The world is not our workshop or testing ground, and there is not some one perspective and way of acting expected of us at each moment. Life has a certain slack to it, "play" in the older sense of looseness or freedom, so that we do not worry about things as much as the serious person. With a sense of humor we are especially well equipped to face new situations, and even failure, with interest, since humor is based on novelty and incongruity, on having one's expectations violated.

The distance in humor, too, gives us a measure of objectivity in looking at ourselves; we see that our own personalities and actions have just as many incongruities in them as anyone else's. Hence we are less egocentric and more realistic in our view of the world. We are more humble in moments of success, less defeated in times of trouble, and in general, more accepting of things the way they are.

This acceptance is especially important in our dealing with other people. When we show people that we have a sense of humor, we let them know that we don't have rigid expectations; they don't have to watch everything they say and every move they make, but can relax and be themselves. It is this aspect of humor, of course, that makes it essential for friendships and marriages.

In the midst of what often seems a pretty rigid world, to conclude, humor offers us flexibility and openness. Not only are we not upset by the incongruities that pervade our lives, but we can actually enjoy them. This is not to say that humor blinds us to the reality of suffering and failure in life, that it deceives us, or "strings us along." Quite the contrary. Humor is not based on false hope—it is not even necessarily optimistic. It does not deny, but affirms the incongruities in things, right down to the fundamental incongruity mentioned earlier "between the eager fret of our life and its final nothingness." Life is still full of predicaments, indeed is itself a kind of predicament. As Woody Allen put it, comparing life to a restaurant, "Not only is the fare lousy, but you get such small portions." And yet, as this comment shows, we can always step back a bit to enjoy the incongruity.

If like Camus we believe that the only really important question is whether we should commit suicide, I think that humor gives us a strong reason for answering No. If only for the amusement it provides, life is worth living. We can even treat the question of suicide with a sense of humor, as Dorothy Parker did:

Razors pain you;
Rivers are damp;
Acids stain you;
And drugs cause cramp.
Guns aren't lawful;
Nooses give;
Gas smells awful;
You might as well live.

# Notes

Chapter 1, pages 1–3

1. Quintilian, "Institutes of the Orator."

Chapter 2, pages 4–14

1. Plato, *Republic*, V, 452; and *Philebus*, 48–50.
2. Cf. Henri Bergson, *Laughter*, in Wylie Sypher, ed., *Comedy* (Garden City: Doubleday Anchor Books, 1956), p. 71: "A comic character is generally comic in proportion to his ignorance of himself."
3. Plato, *Republic*, III, 388.
4. Plato, *Laws*, VII, 816.
5. Ibid., XI, 935–36.
6. Aristotle, *Rhetoric*, II, 12.
7. Aristotle, *Nicomachean Ethics*, IV, 8.
8. Thomas Hobbes, *Leviathan*, in his *Works*, ed. W. Molesworth (London: Bohn, 1839), vol. 3, ch. 11.
9. Hobbes, *Human Nature*, in his *Works*, ed. W. Molesworth (London: Bohn, 1840), vol. 4, ch. 9. Cf. *Leviathan*, ch. 6.
10. Ibid.
11. *Leviathan*, ch. 6.
12. Konrad Lorenz, *On Aggression*, trans. Marjorie Wilson (New York: Harcourt, Brace & World, 1966), pp. 293–97.
13. Anthony Ludovici, *The Secret of Laughter* (New York: Viking Press, 1933), pp. 62–63, 69.

14. Ibid., pp. 98–103.
15. Albert Rapp, *The Origins of Wit and Humor* (New York: E. P. Dutton, 1951).
16. Ibid., p. 21. Cf. Stephen Leacock, *Humor and Humanity* (New York: Holt, 1938), ch. 1.
17. Donald Hayworth, "The Social Origin and Function of Laughter," *Psychological Review*, 35 (1928): 370.
18. Rapp, *Origins of Wit and Humor*, pp. 43–44.
19. Ibid., p. 66.
20. Ibid., p. 68.
21. Voltaire, preface to *L'Enfant Prodigue* (Paris, 1829).
22. Max Eastman, *The Sense of Humor* (New York: Scribner's, 1921), p. 7.
23. Lucien Price, *Dialogues of Alfred North Whitehead* (New York: Mentor Books, 1962), p. 30.
24. J. Huizinga, *Homo Ludens: A Study of the Play-Element in Human Culture* (London: Routledge & Kegan Paul, 1949), pp. 85–86.
25. Two of these studies are discussed in Rapp, *Origins of Wit and Humor*, pp. 34–35.
26. Ibid., p. 67.
27. Hobbes, *Human Nature*, ch. 9, sec. 13.

*Chapter 3, pages 15–19*

1. Quoted in Ludovici, *Secret of Laughter*, p. 27.
2. Aristotle, *Rhetoric*, III, 2.
3. Immanuel Kant, *Kritik of Judgment*, trans. J. H. Bernard (London: Macmillan, 1892), p. 223.
4. Ibid., p. 224.
5. Arthur Schopenhauer, *The World as Will and Idea*, trans. R. B. Haldane and J. Kemp (London: Routledge & Kegan Paul, 1964), vol. 1, ch. 13.
6. Ibid., p. 76.
7. James Beattie, "On Laughter and Ludicrous Composition," in his *Essays*, 3d ed. (London, 1779), p. 304.
8. Ibid., p. 318.
9. Ibid., p. 320.
10. Ibid., p. 305.
11. Ibid., p. 303.
12. Ibid., p. 420.

*Chapter 4, pages 20–37*

1. Lord Shaftesbury, "The Freedom of Wit and Humour," part I, sec. 4, in his *Characteristicks*, 4th ed. (London, 1727), p. 71.

2. Alexander Bain, *The Emotions and the Will*, 3d ed. (London: Longmans & Green, 1875), chs. 10 and 14.
3. Sigmund Freud, *Jokes and Their Relation to the Unconscious*, trans. James Strachey (New York: Penguin Books, 1976), p. 140.
4. Herbert Spencer, "On the Physiology of Laughter," in his *Essays on Education, Etc.* (London: J. M. Dent, 1911).
5. Ibid., p. 299.
6. Ibid., p. 302.
7. See, for example, Wallace L. Chafe, "Humor as a Disabling Mechanism," paper presented at the Second International Conference on Humor, Los Angeles, August 1979.
8. Spencer, "Physiology of Laughter," p. 303.
9. Ibid., p. 304.
10. John Dewey, "The Theory of Emotion," *Psychological Review*, 1 (1894): 559.
11. Freud also published a short essay entitled "Humour," which is found in his *Collected Papers*, vol. 5 (New York: Basic Books, 1959).
12. *Jokes and the Unconscious*, p. 183.
13. Ibid., p. 140.
14. See, e.g., ibid., p. 146.
15. Ibid., pp. 224–25.
16. Ibid., pp. 130–31.
17. Ibid., p. 147; cf. p. 145.
18. Ibid., p. 165.
19. See ibid., ch. 4.
20. Ibid., p. 201; cf. p. 166.
21. Paul Kline, "The Psychoanalytic Theory of Humour and Laughter," in Anthony J. Chapman and Hugh C. Foot, eds., *It's a Funny Thing, Humour.* (papers presented at the International Conference on Humour and Laughter, Cardiff, Wales, July 1976) (Oxford, N.Y.: Pergamon Press, 1977), pp. 10–11.
22. H. J. Eysenck, foreword to Jeffrey H. Goldstein and Paul E. McGhee, eds., *The Psychology of Humor* (New York: Academic Press, 1972), p. xvi.
23. Freud also explains the pleasure of the jest as a saving of psychic energy; see *Jokes and the Unconscious*, pp. 174, 266.
24. Ibid., p. 254.
25. Ibid., p. 255.
26. Ibid., p. 257.
27. Ibid., p. 300.
28. Ibid., pp. 256–57.
29. Ibid., p. 293.
30. Ibid., pp. 295–96.
31. Ibid., p. 295.

*Chapter 5, pages 38–59*

1. Aristotle, *Problems*, XXXV, 6. Cf. Charles Darwin, *The Expression of the Emotions in Man and Animals* (Chicago: University of Chicago Press, 1965), p. 200.
2. Quoted in Max Eastman, *The Sense of Humor* (New York: Scribner's, 1921), pp. 158–59.
3. Jean Piaget, *The Construction of Reality in the Child*, trans. Margaret Cook (New York: Ballantine, 1954), ch. 1.
4. This story is told in James Sully, *An Essay on Laughter* (London: Longmans, Green, 1902), p. 236.
5. Ibid., p. 238.
6. For a fuller account of the development of humor in the child, see Martha Wolfenstein, *Children's Humor* (Glencoe, Ill.: Free Press, 1954); and Paul McGhee, *Humor: Its Origin and Development* (San Francisco: W. H. Freeman, 1979).
7. McGhee, *Humor*, pp. 57–60.
8. Ralph Piddington, *The Psychology of Laughter* (London: Figurehead, 1933), p. 86.
9. Cf. Helmuth Plessner, *Laughing and Crying*, trans. James Spence and Marjorie Grene (Evanston: Northwestern University Press, 1970).
10. L. A. Sroufe and J. C. Wunsch, "The Development of Laughter in the First Year of Life," *Child Development*, 43 (1972): 1326–44.
11. Raymond A. Moody, *Laugh after Laugh* (Jacksonville, Fla.: Headwaters Press, 1978), p. 45.


*Chapter 6, pages 60–84*

1. Quoted in Jacob Levine, ed., *Motivation in Humor* (New York: Atherton Press, 1969), p. 177.
2. Richard Boston, *An Anatomy of Laughter* (London: Collins, 1974), pp. 60–61.
3. I owe this joke to Victor Raskin, who presented it in a paper, "The Linguistic Relativity of Humor," at the Second International Conference on Humor, Los Angeles, August 1979.
4. William Hazlitt, "On Wit and Humour," in *Lectures on the English Comic Writers* (London: Oxford University Press, 1920), Lecture I.
5. John Locke, *An Essay Concerning Human Understanding*, book II, ch. 11, sec. 2.
6. H. P. Grice, "Logic and Conversation," in Peter Cole and Jerry Morgan, eds., *Syntax and Semantics* (New York: Academic Press, 1975), 3: 41–58.

7. David Gordon and George Lakoff, "Conversational Postulates," in Peter Cole and Jerry L. Morgan, eds., *Syntax and Semantics* (New York: Academic Press, 1975), 3: 90.

## Chapter 7, pages 85–100

1. Plato, *Republic*, III, 388.
2. Saint John Chrysostom, *On the Priesthood; Ascetic Treatises; Select Homilies and Letters; Homilies on the Statues*, vol. 9 of *A Select Library of the Nicene and Post-Nicene Fathers of the Christian Church*, ed. Philip Schaff (New York: The Christian Literature Co., 1889), p. 442.
3. Quoted in Ralph Piddington, *The Psychology of Laughter* (London: Figurehead, 1933), p. 158 n. 2.
4. William Prynne, *Histrio-Mastix: the Players Scourge or Actors Tragaedie (London, 1633)*.
5. Lord Chesterfield, *Letters to His Son* (Washington & London: Dunne, 1901), 1: 57–58.
6. Charles Baudelaire, "The Essence of Laughter and More Especially of the Comic in Plastic Arts," in his *The Essence of Laughter and Other Essays, Journals, and Letters*, ed. Peter Quennell (New York: Meridian Books, 1956), p. 113.
7. Ibid., p. 115.
8. Hugues Felicite Robert de Lamennais, *Esquisse d'une Philosophie* (Paris, 1840), book IX, ch. 2, p. 369.
9. George Vasey, *A Philosophy of Laughter and Smiling* (London: J. Burns, 1877), p. 30.
10. Anthony M. Ludovici, *The Secret of Laughter* (New York: Viking Press, 1933), pp. 12–13, 11.
11. See my "Humor and Emotion," forthcoming in *The American Philosophical Quarterly*.
12. George Santayana, *The Sense of Beauty* (New York: Scribner's, 1896), p. 248.

## Chapter 8, pages 101–113

1. Lord Shaftesbury, "The Freedom of Wit and Humour," part 1, sec. 4, in *Characteristicks*, 4th ed. (London, 1727), pp. 71–72.
2. Arthur Schopenhauer, *The World as Will and Idea*, trans. Haldane and Kemp (London: Routledge & Kegan Paul, 1964), 2: 280.
3. Stephen Leacock, *Humor and Humanity* (New York: Henry Holt, 1938), p. 216.
4. Quoted in Horace M. Kallen, *Liberty, Laughter, and Tears* (DeKalb: Northern Illinois University Press, 1968), p. 365.

5. Douglas Lindsey and James Benjamin, "Humor in the Emergency Room: The Etiquette and the Efficacy," presented at the Second International Conference on Humor, Los Angeles, August 1979.

6. Quoted in Max Eastman, *The Sense of Humor* (New York: Scribner's, 1921), p. 188.

7. Viktor Frankl, *The Doctor and the Soul*, trans. Richard and Clara Winston (New York: Alfred Knopf, 1960), pp. 204–15.

8. Allen Fay, *Making Things Better by Making Them Worse* (New York: Hawthorne Books, 1978).

9. Joyce O. Hertzler, *Laughter: A Socio-Scientific Analysis* (New York: Exposition Press, 1970), p. 143.

10. Immanuel Kant, *Kritik of Judgment*, trans. J. H. Bernard (London: Macmillan, 1892), pp. 220–22.

11. See Raymond Moody, *Laugh after Laugh: The Healing Power of Humor* (Jacksonville, Fla.: Headwaters Press, 1978); Norman Cousins, *Anatomy of an Illness as Perceived by the Patient* (New York: Norton, 1979), esp. ch. 1.

12. Cf. Edward Sankowski, "Responsibility of Persons for Their Emotions," *Canadian Journal of Philosophy*, 7 (1977): 829–40.

*Chapter 9, pages 114–120*

1. A. H. Rankin and R. J. Philip, "Epidemic of Laughing in Bukoba District of Tanganyika," *Central African Journal of Medicine*, 9 (1963), quoted in *Newsweek*, 26 August 1963, pp. 74–75.

2. Cf. J. Huizinga, *Homo Ludens: A Study of the Play-Element in Culture* (London: Routledge & Kegan Paul, 1949).

3. William Willeford, *The Fool and His Scepter: A Study in Clowns and Jesters and Their Audience* (Evanston: Northwestern University Press, 1969), pp. 85–87.

4. Ibid., p. 226.

5. Erasmus, *The Praise of Folly*, trans. Hoyt Hopewell Hudson (Princeton: Princeton University Press, 1941), p. 28.

*Chapter 10, pages 121–129*

1. Stephen Leacock, *Humor: Its Theory and Technique* (New York: Dodd, Mead, 1935), p. 4.

2. Aristotle, *Nicomachean Ethics*, X, 6.

3. Cf. Thomas Nagel, "The Absurd," *The Journal of Philosophy*, 68 (1971): 716–27.

4. Friedrich Nietzsche, "On Truth and Falsity in their Ultramoral Sense,"

in his *Complete Works,* ed. Oscar Levy (New York: Russell & Russell, 1964), 2: 173.

5. Stephen Leacock, *Humor and Humanity* (New York: Henry Holt, 1938), pp. 219–20.

6. Elton Trueblood, in *The Humor of Christ* (New York: Harper & Row, 1964), claims that Jesus had a rich sense of humor and was not uniformly serious. To show that Jesus was not above joking, Trueblood cites several passages from the Gospels, such as Jesus' saying that it would be easier for a camel to pass through the eye of a needle than for a rich man to enter Heaven, and Jesus' referring to the Pharisees as "whitewashed tombs." But although the passages cited certainly show that Jesus used inventive metaphors, similes, and other figures of speech, I fail to see how they show any sense of humor in Jesus. Humor requires more than cleverness; it requires a playful attitude toward what one is joking about. Another recent book arguing for the appropriateness of humor in Christianity is Conrad Hyers's *The Comic Vision and the Christian Faith* (New York: Pilgrim Press, 1981). Hyers does an admirable job of expressing the value of the humorous attitude toward life, and tracing his theme through several cultures, works of literature, films, etc. What he utterly fails to do, however, is connect the comic vision with the Jesus of the Gospels or with traditional Christianity.

7. Charles Baudelaire, "The Essence of Laughter and More Especially of the Comic in Plastic Arts," in his *The Essence of Laughter and Other Essays, Journals, and Letters,* ed. Peter Quennell (New York: Meridian Books, 1956), p. 112.

8. Long-Chen-pa, *The Natural Freedom of the Mind (Sems-nyid ngal-gso),* trans. Herbert Guenther, in *Crystal Mirror* (Berkeley, Cal.: Dharma, 1975), 4: 124–25. For an examination of playfulness and humor in Zen Buddhism, see Conrad Hyers, *Zen and the Comic Spirit* (Philadelphia: Westminster, 1973).

# Works Cited

(For a more extensive bibliography on laughter and humor, especially of works in the behavioral sciences, see the bibliography prepared by Jeffrey Goldstein and others in Chapman and Foot, eds., *It's a Funny Thing, Humour* (Oxford, N.Y.: Pergamon Press, 1977), pp. 469–505.

Aristotle. *Nicomachean Ethics.*
———. *Problems.*
———. *Rhetoric.*
Bain, Alexander. *The Emotions and the Will*, 3d ed. London: Longmans & Green, 1875.
Baudelaire, Charles. *The Essence of Laughter and Other Essays, Journals, and Letters.* Ed. Peter Quennell. New York: Meridian Books, 1956.
Beattie, James. "An Essay on Laughter and Ludicrous Composition." In *Essays*, 3d ed. London, 1779.
Bergson, Henri. *Laughter.* In *Comedy*, ed. Wylie Sypher. Garden City: Doubleday Anchor, 1956.
Boston, Richard. *An Anatomy of Laughter.* London: Collins, 1974.
Chapman, Anthony, and Foot, Hugh, eds. *It's a Funny Thing, Humour.* Oxford, N.Y.: Pergamon Press, 1977.
Chesterfield, Lord. *Letters to His Son.* Washington and London: Dunne, 1901.
Chrysostom, St. John. *On the Priesthood; Ascetic Treatises; Select Homilies and Letters; Homilies on the Statues. A Select Library of the*

*Nicene and Post-Nicene Fathers of the Christian Church*, ed. Philip Schaff, vol. 9. New York: The Christian Literature Co., 1889.

Cousins, Norman. *Anatomy of an Illness as Perceived by the Patient*. New York: Norton, 1979.

Darwin, Charles. *The Expression of the Emotions in Man and Animals*. Chicago: University of Chicago Press, 1965.

de Lamennais, Hugo. *Esquisse d'une Philosophie*. Paris, 1840.

Dewey, John. "The Theory of Emotion." *Psychological Review*, 1 (1894): 553–69.

Eastman, Max. *The Sense of Humor*. New York: Scribner's, 1921.

Erasmus. *In Praise of Folly*, trans. Hoyt Hopewell Hudson. Princeton: Princeton University Press, 1941.

Eysenck, H. J. Foreword to *Psychology of Humor*, ed. Goldstein and McGhee.

Fay, Allen. *Making Things Better by Making Them Worse*. New York: Hawthorn, 1978.

Frankl, Viktor. *The Doctor and the Soul*, trans. Richard and Clara Winston. New York: Alfred Knopf, 1960.

Freud, Sigmund. "Humor." *Collected Papers*, vol. 5. New York: Basic Books, 1959.

———. *Jokes and Their Relation to the Unconscious*, trans. and ed. James Strachey. Harmondsworth: Penguin, 1976.

Goldstein, Jeffrey, and McGhee, Paul, eds. *The Psychology of Humor*. New York: Academic Press, 1972.

Gordon, David, and Lakoff, George. "Conversational Postulates." *Syntax and Semantics*, vol. 3, ed. Peter Cole and Jerry Morgan. New York: Academic Press, pp. 83–106.

Grice, H. P. "Logic and Conversation." *Syntax and Semantics*, vol. 3, ed. Peter Cole and Jerry Morgan. New York: Academic Press, pp. 41–58.

Hayworth, Donald. "The Social Origin and Function of Laughter." *Psychological Review*, 35 (1928): 367–84.

Hazlitt, William. *Lectures on the English Comic Writers*. London: Oxford University Press, 1920.

Hertzler, Joyce. *Laughter: A Socio-Scientific Analysis*. New York: Exposition Press, 1970.

Hobbes, Thomas. *Human Nature. English Works*, vol. 4, ed. Molesworth. London: Bohn, 1840.

———. *Leviathan. English Works*, vol. 3, ed. Molesworth. London: Bohn, 1839.

Huizinga, J. *Homo Ludens: A Study of the Play-Element in Human Culture*. London: Routledge & Kegan Paul, 1949.

Hyers, Conrad. *The Comic Vision and the Christian Faith*. New York: Pilgrim Press, 1981.

————. *Zen and the Comic Spirit.* Philadelphia: Westminster, 1973.

Kallen, Horace. *Liberty, Laughter and Tears.* DeKalb: Northern Illinois University Press, 1968.

Kant, Immanuel. *Kritik of Judgment,* trans. J. H. Bernard. London: Macmillan, 1892.

Kline, Paul. "The Psychoanalytic Theory of Humour and Laughter." *It's a Funny Thing, Humour,* eds. Chapman and Foot, pp. 7–12.

Leacock, Stephen. *Humor and Humanity.* New York: Holt, 1938.

————. *Humor: Its Theory and Technique.* New York: Dodd, Mead, 1935.

Levine, Jacob, ed. *Motivation in Humor.* New York: Atherton Press, 1969.

Locke, John. *An Essay Concerning Human Understanding,* ed. Peter Nidditch. New York: Oxford University Press, 1979.

Long-Chen-pa. *The Natural Freedom of the Mind (Sems-nyid ngalgso),* Trans. Herbert Guenther. *Crystal Mirror,* vol. 4. Berkeley, Cal.: Dharma Publishing, 1975.

Lorenz, Konrad. *On Aggression,* trans. Marjorie Wilson. New York: Harcourt, Brace & World, 1966.

Ludovici, Anthony. *The Secret of Laughter.* New York: Viking, 1933.

McGhee, Paul. *Humor: Its Origin and Development.* San Francisco: W. H. Freeman, 1979.

————, ed. *The Psychology of Humor.* New York: Academic Press, 1972.

Moody, Raymond. *Laugh after Laugh.* Jacksonville, Fla.: Headwaters Press, 1978.

Morreall, John. "Humor and Emotion." *The American Philosophical Quarterly,* forthcoming.

Nagel, Thomas. "The Absurd." *The Journal of Philosophy,* 68 (1971): 716–27.

Nietzsche, Friedrich. "On Truth and Falsity in Their Ultramoral Sense." *Complete Works,* ed. Oscar Levy, vol. 2. New York: Russell & Russell, 1964, pp. 173–92.

Piaget, Jean. *The Construction of Reality in the Child,* trans. Margaret Cook. New York: Ballantine, 1954.

Piddington, Ralph. *The Psychology of Laughter.* London: Figurehead, 1933.

Plato. *Laws.*

————. *Philebus.*

————. *Republic.*

Plessner, Helmuth. *Laughing and Crying,* trans. James Spence and Marjorie Grene. Evanston: Northwestern University Press, 1970.

Prynne, William. *Histrio-Mastix: The Players Scourge or Actors Tragaedie.* London, 1633.

Rankin, A. H., and Philip, R. J. "Epidemic of Laughing in Bukoba District of Tanganyika." *Central African Journal of Medicine,* 9 (1963). Quoted in *Newsweek,* 26 August 1963, pp. 74–75.

Rapp, Albert. *The Origins of Wit and Humor.* New York: E. P. Dutton, 1951.

Sankowski, Edward. "Responsibility of Persons for Their Emotions." *Canadian Journal of Philosophy,* 7 (1977), 829–40.

Santayana, George. *The Sense of Beauty.* New York: Scribner's, 1896.

Schopenhauer, Arthur. *The World as Will and Idea,* trans. R. B. Haldane and J. Kemp. London: Routledge & Kegan Paul, 1964.

Shaftesbury, Lord. "The Freedom of Wit and Humour." *Characteristicks,* 4th ed. London, 1727.

Spencer, Herbert. "On the Physiology of Laughter." *Essays on Education, Etc.* London: Dent, 1911, pp. 298–309.

Sroufe, L. A., and Wunsch, J. C. "The Development of Laughter in the First Year of Life." *Child Development,* 43 (1972): 1326–44.

Sully, James. *An Essay on Laughter.* London: Longmans, Green, 1902.

Trueblood, Elton. *The Humor of Christ.* New York: Harper & Row, 1964.

Vasey, George. *The Philosophy of Laughter and Smiling,* 2d ed. London: J. Burns, 1877.

Voltaire, Francois. Preface to *L'Enfant Prodigue.* Paris, 1829.

Willeford, William. *The Fool and His Scepter: A Study in Clowns and Jesters and Their Audience.* Evanston: Northwestern University Press, 1969.

Wolfenstein, Martha. *Children's Humor.* Glencoe, Ill.: Free Press, 1954.

# Index

# Index

## Index